Cries of somewhere's soil

Poetry

Thibault Jacquot-Paratte

Seeing the land, <u>who</u> has suffered some great losses,
the possibility of establishment,
is a dared-to-dream, and a river.
And in my latest dreams of "it was so hot the day I left"
and "weather was bone dry"
I do perceive a banjo singer,
General Custer dripping under a little, a big horn,
the forehead and the blood of the buffalo
how could this land(, has) suffered some great losses
a skull under the daylight of the prairies
coyotes in the night hollering
I never perceived them as such a threat.
I hung it on my wall to scare away the tourist,
and desirous of the kind of mesquite,
which inflames my pallet and yet tastes so sweet,
perhaps the valley is so far, the wall with an aztec name,
no relative have been the same,
the rifle which shoots today and dies tomorrow,
living in the mountains remain with no sorrow for colonialists
the shepherds' lead their herds here and there,
dogs at their heads unlike the dragons of the north mens' travels,
slobbering treachery of Geronimo; here comes the bride,
seeing the land who has suffered some great losses,
to whom to California crosses, and then stays far away.

And the youth growls
savanna sunrise the beasts they smile
the rabbits in their country corn.
At a child once a five foot six
a growth spurt day might be surprise
but hoped it to you cannot shrink
what to hope to do?
To say yes the opened spaces
cry out and say my name
the mountains on foot we climb their top,
cry out and say my name.
Could you think of such inconveniences
I palp the sound at heart
through some displease some part
at 40 is good time
at now what yell is passion filled
cry out and say my name,
the inches taken won't be killed,
compressed a very old man,
my growl it warns a might be coming
a might be nevermore
A growl 'tis there 'tis height and size,
return the favour a precised
cry out and say my name
I have wept on yours.

I stepped away to the middle of the night
out of the closet or out the door
to meet with the hobo crying in the street
on a bed of his money and his booze
there could always be number two
there could always be the
unspoken, unwritten connection,
unanswered messages
Flagpoles left unbannered,
bare simplicity of grey matter,
Aluminum, the gaps of the earth, rock particles,
the sobbing on the concrete, splat,
the resting bet and when the clouds calm to fog,
we will be resuming our journey,
and your hands dry my tears.

I would not lay any regrets staying awoken by meaningless love
till the early A.M.
Knowing in the past as I now have
and that of which desire you feed
I have not refused nice, not satisfied need
he who has satisfied
he who does not look blankly at shame
I would not hold any grudge and not remember her name
simply recall her American heartbeat on my bare chest in the dark
night,
warm of so many sea currents
I would not lay any longer
the tide of whoring haven a long time gone,
a long time left, now headed lost,
to the coastal, oil spills coast of purity ring
(I would not lay any regrets, staying awoken by meaningless love
till the early A.M.)

Have you been insane to say what has crossed
And what (have) has (did) crossed
Your legs which have walked from near, semi birth
To your age which has ushered suppose-to-be new
Mentalities (have they reflected how you feel,
Or has the pragmatism of the made look stiff halted
Has it broken all the surrealism of affection)
Just imagine all the neck's wasted time to have

Could it be that animals are the romantics
As the caveman reaches out when please
And as our people chose soap

In the tulips the, mole is happy
Its little beady eyes in the sock(its nature
It is pure and odes but concern of the moment, and none of)
Children they gather around to hear his story
Elders they ask louder to hear his story
Adults they think telling youngens this story
Teenagers, they leave, for they don't care the story
Is told all they all miss out, but those
Un-understanding their own goal
Doeth thee need to be returned at 5 (
To take 5 or 6 and seven whatever age you wish,
Whatever to distillate you're pupils
And to let the sun shine in for that the colours should either blind
Or give a pretty veil reflections vibrations rejected by things,
 Accepted by you

oh what a fool I am,
to believe in the luck of clothing
and to wear another's skin
it would only be some sort of warmth
left by almost freezing nights
embraced and awaken
there are semi-precious stones in the morning light,
as under the earth's crust

oh father, forget what's in the
and the ever growing
and the black thorn bushes
blood drips worry not,
I have some napkin in my back pocket dear, worry not.
And father, there is a rose
a rose of the purest colour
a rose of the softest petals
and yes, the most fragile heart,
and luckily,
some seeds may fall somewheres.

Night that has become of me,
as to be on your bed an intruder
of natural place and of natural order,
no horizon now can see.

now, I am drunk and tired and pissed off
and I want to leave for France
and I do not have to see her face
nor yours but I will
and I want to leave for France
want to see again something gives and goes
and I want to leave for France
and I've seen enough, I've talked enough
I want to leave for France
you know a ship, a boat, a drink
better luck in there even if it were to sink,

I want to leave for France;
under a wool blanket in the stormy night of rain,
and I want to leave for France,
maybe in there I might live once again
I want to leave for France.

now when you drive off into that Texan landscape and
and you got that big red sun beating off into your eyes,
and I do mean beating off as its results hits you in warm and
personal oblivion
eradication of ways and ignoring tenderness of afternoon groves,
with the shade of the oaks, and the pines, and of beech
and the branches swaying in the Tennessee fashion
where the mountains grow up and down and you chase like the
lion down south
yet going west you got that landscape,
you got the sand dunes in the flat miles going on and rolling,
and sometimes you got those mountains but with no shade,
you got those mountains in the hard and heavy rocky formations;
and the best *tyme* and the memories like the tombstone ten gallon
and leather suits
the memorabilia photography, the smoky gas station images with
the chained dogs
and the old rusty tanker trucks sitting there for god who know's long
the reaching for the sky industrial paint white propane gas tank,
and an old manual pump where you pay inside, you prepay the gas, and
you activate that lever
you pull on it and the gas may boost your movement towards the fiery
bright setting day
and the horizon which is growing to a dim dark black and hellfire red
and the nuances of blindness; you are thankful for the opposite headlights,
and you may stop until nighttime when there is and infinite and eternal veil
wherever you may look you see the stars and the light moon light blue
the earth is black and rich land as the old lightning use to say,
lord, that is rich land,
and sometimes there is a hole in the sky wherever the foundations
of mankind are distracted,
and yet you keep on rolling eighty miles an hour or more in free

range country,
and your headlights are rewarded by nice golden ribbon,
and the land is so wide and vast a nighttime roller like you is rare,
you may cross a pickup or semi-truck carrying its load in the new continent,
carrying its own worth in the consumption of man kind's only wish and goal
-      to live an easy fun filled life,
and I always said I could be a trucker, for I need no sleep but the bare minimum,
and the early dusk to dawn air is all I crave, from cold mountain air,
because you know that in the desert you can feel the sun -
and the sand keeps no heat, you can feel that first ray coming up on the land and hitting you
with which you yelp "yee-haw", looting about in the shrubbery bushes and a fresh harvest of nopalitos,
and you salute a friendly mexicano man with whom you share the land
-

now to drive up my dear flowers with roots so light,
with the whatever type of birds, I just know they ain't buzzards
I just want to now, and drive up until my death in through the deep Texan landscape,
 all though that ain't my name.

Yet I miss my fair Irish maiden,
her hair curls of how I'm locked
entangled in some net between
do not hang me my dear, I'm with you forever in any case,
for the Irish have eyes of songs
they have treasures in their language
saved from flames and barbarians
history has been their friend
and they have pride
for Kells is a drawing of a great
there is reading and advancement
moving forward is a thing re-Joyce
her tongue has claimed my mouth more than once
I dare say have appreciated it
the bumps along the way as a rocky month-of-may
roads, carrying buddies along the cobbled streets,
believe me her deep blue soul is waiting somewhere
and a *dia duich* awaits I say, I wait to say merry
they have good cider I'll add
and I've been happy elsewhere
I've studied with legendary minds and the winds of Siberia
I've kissed many another and the beds' squeaks behind
we've not talked in person yet my letters reach,
she has taken some time to answer,
afoot most of the forests have let me live through
wolves have howled with me
and away shall we go to forget a past we don't want to admit,
and yet I miss my fair Irish maiden,
perhaps this April I shall go back.

A harvest is but,
        and the lengthy virtuoso,
      and the calling of a woman on a back porch,
            her voice caries off in the distance, yelling
                  "come home, come home"
                all to her son, she can see him running
downhill in the glacier valley,
                "come home, come home"
                  "it's getting dark and you should not roam-
      – for there is something that lurks about
-       and in the sailor's tongue no doubt,
-       the red lights are light and sights
          the gun shots aimed at the thief in the condemning cold air,
              do not wait to be hot,
                    and to them it's synonymous in jail,
                      do not run towards a cell,
                but stay and hear my bell to which pious
kneel and pray,
                come home, come home"
but we have eaten,
and we did sing,
but now we go to hunt and bring-
-and bring back in ever more,
the meat of our nights as here is boar.

to\ b\u\y\e buye,
consume a departure like the trip of the strongest drugs
- mourning is never a new dawn,
fell and feel the rain on the skin of a new soul -
the gust of wind is a sun swept heather
its perfume hidden as a shy smile,
a woman's smile as it climbs timidly on the side of a face,
and in the dank corners where lovers make love.

In the airport terminal sounds are lost,
and our empty eyes gaze forwardly
carpets are clouds and we stress somehow
forgetting all that is the cherished and behold
hatred may vanish once more and always
forget where you come from, and speak now with grace
forget where your home is, read not that page -
as far as they know you are a prophet,
a celestial being, and you descend from the stars.

And you have left where you came from,
you are in something new,
a taste may be acquired or of some sort fatigue,
feel the rain on your face, that is all you should do,
above all, and all else that is all you may need -
bleed my son, bleed;
and build by yourself,
whatever it may be it will stick and will see
and a scar on your hands and your need,
say adios and ingest
of your tree, here, the seed.

My momma said to be standing on the back porch
and I ran through the tall *grasses* with the grain silos like
sun table, solar turntables, turning in a hip hop beat
I hear some bass in her lower regions
and touching me touching her she touches me as I want her
she is who ever I may cross,
 'cause my momma told me, my momma told me
I was the prettiest boy around -
as if again we told ourselves looking into the mirror;
and then I got to New York city
or some sort of orgy
and I spent more time in the bronx than I did getting rich
the bridge of Brooklyn is my greatest achievement
I crossed it so many times
trying to reach some sort of corn field
and listen to the code of the streets
and rise to the trumpets
Shakespeare rolls over in his grave
he would steal your rhymes like some museum curator
let me touch your head for I am the re-animator
and let me swim without alligators
there is no difference between the subways and the sewers
the time the next hurricane hits no repairs will be made
wear your beanie and mits and stay warm in the wait
rode my bicycle down the bells ringing for my life and my past
colonial motherfuckers gave me my faith and I follow its teachings
and colonial thinking has become my thinking I am from Liberia
motherfucker.
And glorified father figures, my momma told me,
don't be so negative
there is always some five million dollar bridge I can sleep under

why sleep in a five hundred thousand bucks worth apartment
time is just there to be talking with you
talking with you and touching your hips dancing some fly salsa
dancing
and your hips they drive me as crazy as your cheeks are kissable
my lips are the pavement whore, the have-laid
and the have-heard even more scary stories than the children
hiding under the sink
because their mamma was screaming and making love to a serial killer,
and my momma told me, my momma told me
and I ran through all those fields
to become the man whore that I am
and I would take any love as I would eat any pie feeling ill from
some dope I thought I would like
and I will take some again soon
and thats at three AM and the waitress is pretty
and she is wearing some blue dress I would proudly rip in some
passionate love
the counter is so clean
the fork is in my mouth
I am eating this delicious piece of pie
and my momma told me
don't miss out on what you like.
Goodbye cruel world and happy new year's.
You may find somme black apartment
that's ok, I'm not hungry anymore
before, making food became my life
; I work as a cook and I like the back alley like a breeze of fresh air
there are some milk crates I can sit on
and the grass they grow and I run through
picking potatoes and cutting off their leaves
and in my dreams she is standing next to me

she is holding a bong pipe and looks so sweet
her eyes are sweet and empty, and I try to get up to meet her
and my momma always told me
never get lost and don't be a beggar.
one more, often, then doesn't, often leads to more
let me kiss her and it won't restore
often leads, often leads to more
let me be the biggest kid next door
who is often the bully or the best friend
let me be the bass player, the pivoting point
let me be quite more
then again, then again, let me be the end
let me talk about the air which is so moist and so damn moist
you know what I mean when the guns are so cold they rust
let me tell you I like to lay back and look up at the stars
there are no better stars than above the dampest sea
the day tomorrow there will be a storm.
She is the nicest good looking and I've been gone so long
let me yell "damn it" and disasters swipe their credit cards around
the globe
all the time bro, let me – the winter has been a quite lovely season
with clear blue skies they make me want to speak german
so simple, so simply be mine in the disgusting disappearing and
dim twilight
and I will find the piece of a star
behind a fallen tree.
And don't understand
but I will eat it with a glass of milk;
my momma told me -
as I ran away, slowly, and I ran away; slowly.

Crossings with dates in my hands -
with clusters of dates in theirs bright yellow coronation
in my hands, and with the hard hitting boxer of a so\un
so one day he went up and became a star
so small to literature students
who really cares, he is like an interpret
in some books are written the names of fifth century actors,
in their days were surely important
but what is there to stay
hit me hard today - my bruise will heal.
The nile river has become so polluted and yet we fish
as the *pregos* and *you're-welcomes* are not allowed to eat from
the baltic sea
and I've crossed some dunes to reach the salt
they were pink and made up of coral
and I can still talk to some girl
who, she, regrets her lost learnings
I have dates, I have mandarines, I have a cart full of passed days
and cargo ships take some of me

drink it while it's warm
because it's hot, because it's liquid
you will be thirsty
and it won't make you sick.
Have you crossed the town of Badwatter and wondered how they
lived?
Have you been the hobo who fills his jugs
on this they are generous
to let us fill our recipients
and drink it because it's cool and the sun is beating down
when the snow will be falling
the water harvesters waiting for ice to drip
and who will make fire
to drink it while it's warm
and because it's warm.

I like the place with the hung woman
if you go back to the harps
playing strings in gospel mementos
take me down to some lonesome valley
sang her last word in my ears
if only I could see
one last sight
her death bed is a monster
and a lie
her monster is a lie
that room where she hung herself
I might still feel her presence
if I sit very quietly
and do not cry.

We are so young, and life seems so distant,
and I cannot imagine where your face will become
what its colour and what its subtlety
will it still be in some royalty
look out for the ghosts of some same house.
And I have a spot on my upper left cheek
the life of wine is a chalice of bright red silk
and it evolves as lightly tapping theatre
or that time we went out to the ballet
when the author was our age
between hope, and hedonists and *yolo*
beware my dear, and sleep in my arms
and we will get through this
thinking that we are still
 somewhere between ten and twenty years of age,
all I would want
is for tenderness to bloom.

crowns have been chased away
bows down to this day to a will,
and a governing force
which has made mistakes in the raging Struen-*see*
navigating further may it be,
to control our every move,
or to be stronger, simply.
May we never again kill,
a comrade;
we would not want to read our loss
in tomorrow's ready newspapers.
be informed my former loved ones,
carrying on with thoughtless ways
may we once more cheer on our nation's flag
floating above the parliamentary building,
cheering on our people's elected representatives

Supposedly they have seen me before
but above all do not forget
clock towers in the everyday cold
tell her what to do but it's louder than your voice
call on easier time
yell to the mountains and see parts crumble
danger, danger calls out the dagger in your beating bosom
won't you come along the river banks
every little wave
is a word
you will never hear again.
And supposedly, supposedly
I would like to see you again,
and supposedly, supposedly
estimates will be correct
answers will be truthful
and jails will be filled

My dog, you know, he's my only friend as we keep each other warm in the winter months, as we roam the streets by day or night, and as I try to split the coins we earn in an old coffee cup I picked up on the street into a meal we can both eat, we can share, and sometimes I give him a little more than I take. We can talk together. There are crazy hobos, there are drunken hobos and there are hobos full of drugs. there a dangerous hobos and there are fake hobos with their fifty dollar shoes. I'm a hobo with a dog and he is my only friend.

Some dark beast has been clawing out my insides
and has been tossing, no more than shards of the diamond shape
lively and crystallized human life
I am, no more than a fossil
and its eyes are staring right at me, they are staring
sparkling like not much has, ever or before,
I am lying back to the floor
it is ripping out my, most profound
its fur is of smoke
the, black and beautiful and the dense of the fires I made,
out of anything.
I am made out of anything.
And sometimes a shovel may hit an ancient,
and a most secret cemetery,
projecting the laughing demon into the air
if no fire comes down
should we have a gut scare,
because I love you
and I've made love to no one else.
And some canine on his hind legs and his claws deep in my stomach.
And some dark beast his eyes staring me down
his eyes are cold and damp
and you know a tramp
runs away from such hunters
they pray the weak as I
how on their backs they scream and lie
and have been liars to mostly themselves
and who have not listened, who have been so def
and who now have around the corner,
the voice and or, the smell of her
ride on and do not die a death like me

eaten by a beast who needs not be.
and love is not not-having any feelings for anyone else

love is going against those feelings
because what you have is so dear to you
that you would rather keep it
-than to gamble all of it in some high hopes in which,
in the end,
you will probably miss what you had,
because you had love.

What good is sleep in any ways,
tomorrow is a day of nothing more
and if I get up out of bed
to lay my feet upon the floor
where to go to keep me fed
to work to wander the road amazed
in my eyes and the wind so thrill
a fishing line to hook again
a man with hope to see what will
but again feel the hours of night
which mostly too fast sometimes spill
and I will wait with my dear friends
here at the bus station
until I wait, until what ends
what good is sleep for now begone,
and the sun will rise.

Capitalism is (wearing me, -
It has bought my skin off my flesh and bones -
down)
in my heart filled with paint
it was on sale, and it does not drip
as the perfection of technologies is a motivation
 - so is the need for improvement
and so we go forward in time
the broken pieces keep the stronger going
the wheelchairs of large companies have abolished stairs
and our scalps before our hair
syringes ready for action
straps of leather on our chairs
before the tv's lay out the stories
which rumour the ways and roads
that school is bad for young children,
and that it will protect them from the dangers of reading.
(under the bridges
watchmakers keep going the course
and measure how long
and see how well you fare,
loafing out with bare feet
the capital city is large and wide.)
I got lost in the streets of Washington and took a piss in a subur-
ban avenue
doctor of medicine, I stride in and out of the monuments
capital city. I see you as my lovely wife
and bring you, as I go
different perspectives some time will be ago.
Parking is hard to find
I have no spare change

the street cleaners will clean my car away;
capital city, you have your ways, and I stroll around.
Take a picture of me with the poor old bag-lady
she is so fractured and miserable with bills on her face,
She has such a poor outstanding debt
let me touch oiled soil and soiled earth by gases and oil
there use to be easier ways to keep yourself warm
and I can just lay out in the sun
every weekend
if only from the pawnshop
I can get my skin and flesh
back onto my bones!

Capital city I heard you flashing laws
who does it protect and where's the cash to?
Why do the big companies get what they don't need?
In the summertime I'm thumbing around
going to California to send some back home
the dust is in my old stagnant eyes
statue on the mantel
the living room is a place of many comforts
the ones and the others chat and drink tea
and I watch them
there is no drink for me.
Capital city is a place of safe respite
she is my good luck lady
I paint her on the side of my airplane with lovely long legs
her hair is in the wind; it is some sort of golden blond
let me present myself a hero
from the Appalachian trail
swimming in the great lakes
when it rains in the Yukon
when you're down and out,

when it rains on the capital city,
I'll still be loving you,
bumming around elsewhere,
a chic at my arms
and she will be all
capitalism (I'll be wearing)
nobody wants to be the outsider
when they have no priorities in life.

Capital city, is the most important thing
and to you, to me, to the others,
to say we love and cheat on thee?
And down down, to the last and the latest
news flash
lightning bolts
some have a lightning rod and thunder bays
on the edges of great and windy,
cold, clammy, glaciers of lakes,
with forests, repetitions and repetitions
history first met you since forever
you have not evolved and perhaps at best became a puddle of
navigable water
and this time I'm drowning,
if not only because I never learned to swim,
down into its dark and icy debts.
I've heard rumours of there being sharks
and the Ogopogo might rise up and snatch children
make your way over the mountains,
in the midsts of rock giants' fights
never again praise the golden coin
but the road which leads there, dear, costs full of regrets
in the chest there is no comparison,
finding a resting place

speak as you will,
but not at our customs.

Putting on something fierce
backpacks filled with stones, training the inquisition
some moral
national ideology
portrait of a perfect man
putting off every other thought
to be shocked sooner, or to be shocked never,
can one be avoided,
is a goal of a lifetime
and goal, which has bought such effort,
and as to risk!

The citadel is the mother of books
tell me whether or not you want to see
my underpants, and we could arrange
in the back of some van, call me a prostitute
is a job I would gladly do
and to sell what is inside of you,
it's barely different from what we've done before
have you read what's in tuna? Its disgusting!
Full of mercury and lead,
never again in my day
shall we vote for who once was on our side?
Shall we vote for the ones who stayed?

Capital city my mistress of somewhat affaires
I prance in your shabby streets,
acting like nothing before the police officers who are on service
acting like a hooker for the police officers on break
my shaven legs may appeal your gaze

you know yourself what you can win
capitalism and citadel of former hopes
machinery of insolence
process of elimination
resilience is a virtue if you have never before tried
who never again cared for aged art
fractured partitions which can be picked up
people rap over Beethoven's ninth
call me whenever you are done so we can discuss a sense in your
words
again and against, capital city
let me wonder your matured streets
in your basement lies the screaming subway where bums go to
sleep at night
to kick them all out would be a travesty and an insult
you give no other shelter
yet those tunnels belong to you, ô capital city
let me see the hands hidden behind your back,
try asking me the same thing
let us play paddy cakes and see where this leads on,
a relationship once we grow up;
capital city, let your lights burn a little longer,
once again we could have a correspondence
following you up in the news papers
and I will fill my water bottle in the sink of gas stations and
highway pit-spots,
capital city my beard itches
capital city where are cures?
I may watch baseball if only I could joint it with diabetic beer
bare with me, we all like to be drunk,
I have been so with you more than once, capital city.

Never amounting to nothing,
capital city am I yours?
I've beaten stone with an old hammer,
and I've seen myself crack under pressure.
If I chose back-breaking jobs that no one else wants,
I'd be expecting to get paid more than what they don't need
why would mining coal underground with the asthmatic pounds,
rhythm of the folksongs, roughneck and carts of black fossils
would filling out a paper be a less envied destiny?
I would pick up a pen as I raise two handedly this pickaxe
breaking the chains of you, capital city
riding up and down the streets in a taxi cab and a suit
with a banjo on my knee, capital city,
separated again, understand first world, third world
eating a slice of apple pie call me Davy Crocket,
opposing the president for equality in India rights
born to climb into a suit of everything used
I picked the bones clean off of this here deer
its antlers in a fire, I have others over my mantel,
decoratings over for the Christmas season
commercials have brought my sons to this thing they'll never use
you could always market such things as books
as in between catches when the fish barely bite
the peace and quiet keeps my troubles away,
I have a story here to help in that said
capital city I vote during every election;
I have seen you every year during, capital city
Let me tell you, let's trade places
let us do that for a week
- you CEO, I want to see you here
let me see you next to the track
hear that whistling
the conductor is somewhere an employee you rely on

we have a term: it's "obsolete" -
that means if we wouldn't need him, he'd ain't be here.

Listen to me capital city with a mask of my face and Nixon in
your pocket
dial your phone and call your friends
we will have a party all together
mine will be there to sing
on the avenues with leafless trees
industrial smoke rising over the concrete rooftops
humidity of the pavement and street cleaner clean the filth
capital city, open the office windows and let in the streams of
hose-running tap water
capital city with a 70% off sale
with a loss in profit, never in your lifetime
with a solid profit on a 70% off sale
decrease your hopes and dreams with pretty things
where is the latest job do you think -
do not lay there busted with a sold home and a hook in your hand
crying the yo-ho chanteys and sail away the seas
capital city a floating sail in the
wreckage of the last war
a message in the people's eye
a black flag with a skull and bones
a scream and "man the stations"
protect yourself from the assailants
yet masked with scarves and an eye-patch
is the bearded buccaneer a neat foreign devil
is his tongue your neighboured cousin
son of an immigrant's grand-daughter
raising heck in his bankruptcy scare
lord this land will have an exile
the ships are ready from Boston,

the airplanes from the terrible rumours of Denver
who died in Denver and waited in vain
who will do the same in Maine
have you been to the north of that state?

Capitalism in western-latin writing
capitalism with a "C" and two "I"'s, now isn't that ironic?
Capital city with something to say,
you with a hat to judge the people's way
wearing me, stomach and all -
having a good time at a wiener roast
enjoying the hot-dog I just ate
my stomach pumped clean
at least I will be lean and fat free;
what do they do with that they take out?

Capital city to the rhythm of mighty, sexual Jazz
cracking out on movement and speeded ignorance
capitalism in western novels and new philosophy
to slow down is something is and to envy
they all wish, and watch, and go back to their heart attacks

Capital City I see your boutiques and their shirts and suits,
two are the same with the suitcases of dollar bills
may they fly and paste themselves on the pavement,
on the location,
on the claims of crime-free, no pressure environment
gangsters with pants to their ankles, gangsters with belts and
bracers
gangsters with empty violin coffins and gagsters with a beat-box
listen, the yo-yo care free glow of the yuppie attitude
with money to spare and a *save the whales* shirt
read the label they say, they have that right, read the label

the price of turf is the open market "what the fuck"
and so they open malls outside of the city,
where the spaces are large and to park is easy;
oh capital city, your ruined hopes
your merchants away and in the suburbs live the every family,
and inside your waist's perimeter:
offices of lawyers, insurance cabinets, private medical clinics
with a cynical laughter, capital city, with a cynical smirk
riding the child ferris wheel of child want
a candy apple you will not eat
a giant stuffed dog,
won with many a wasted dollar from a ripoff game
shooting glass bottles with light, used, screwed-unscrewed corks
bouncing off them a million with the participant frustrated
cussing shenanigans at the unwashed Carney with his rotten lead teeth
hissing a plump laugh of every now and then average on the job,
handing the fake pup with a participation prize excuse
shoving the useless bullets back into their pressurized tubes
waiting for the next hand holding daddy
saying "will you win this for your sweetheart little angel?"
capital city, with an eye full, golden ocean of the city lights
wishing the palace of king tsars and other dead folks
hanging the amber chandeliers above your golden jewelled crown
even with news of the western front
vast, unhappy soldiers and grunts and indecisive, disagreement of
populations
ferris wheel or balcony,
run my liege, run
run capital city, and drop your kingdom of,
certainly kind, and unlikely to displease more than ninety-so
percent,
run, your camouflage does not work anymore,
run, flee, if not from me,

from the bacterial infection rummaging through your scorched skin,
capital city,
run and come back, new, feeling better,
liberated from all the carbon-monoxide and co2 alike
go to the doctors in the White House and on Parliament Hill
go to the Red Square and have a discussion with Putin,
go to all the things and have a meeting with the Nordic Council,
certainly Athena would have a word or two,
a word through her statue who, her either, has not moved in
millionaires
and bank accounts rummaging through type-writers,
accusing every one who doesn't agree of being a communist,
of being a fascist pig and a foreign devil just like you stereotype
the rest
capital city, in your mafia's local barber there is bound to be a
mirror as well,
look as you sit,
a razor to your not yet slit throat,
capital city, step out of the closet
wear the clothes you have always wanted to wear,
read a book capital city, read a book for all and everyone
start out small or with the morning paper
there should be no affiliation with information,
give it to me like its, pro's and con's
let there be all there is to hear,
the public will decide of what goes in their ears
the dangers of pro's and the pro's of con's
and if I repeated myself too much in my choice of words
there is no problem capital city
I will not rephrase but let you read it again,
and again and again,
so you can find out what you can,
so you can find out, capital city;

the homeless, have they a name,
raining on their unsheltered heads
leaning towards low ends,
drowning in flash stock-market
floods and crashes, the men in suits
rummaging through ideals and the lives of peasantry
did you ever consider meeting
chronicles of demise
capital city,
open your eyes and rub off the corners filled with sleep
she has walked upon your streets
she is already here,
don't you hear
your economies and dare-to-cling hands on knotted ties
iron grips, sauntering irons jetting their pale blue flames on your
fingers
they may dare never to move again,
nor to kiss a lady's hand, nor to propose to be engaged
to dance a slow dance with a frozen stiff neck
to breath in warm skin's scent
to find the same in a freshly dry-cleaned suit
touch the lining of her neatly chosen dress
but capital city, tell me what do you want?
Where does the world turn and where is your home
is the flag which waves waging its ever loyal tale in the gazing wind
the Frisbee throwing hands placed on a barely beating diabetic chest,
with cholesterol and all the modern problems of not walking with
our four legged,
four legged position, barking and spanking,
not walking and not dancing
do not worry your over thinking mind
(you may have a) – stroke the soft fur of your lap-lying tricolour
company

caress the yapping, barking, having an orgasm
masturbate the erected penis
(of some fellow bank owner to send him the message as well) -
and, for gods' sakes, ask the question, god fearing
was it so complicated?

Capitalism is smoking some pipe someplace and is hiding its
shaggy face
and has smoke coming from its comical ears and rummy's red nose
makes some farce about making it big and the way it already rose
it looks at itself in a bus stop mirror and calls for a bank account
to put all its silver
it pulls out its hair and hopes to make one-percent interest
with high hopes it eagerly awaits,
better have shaved it off for the victims of cancer
it has a look in its dark-circles-under-eyes
bickering black and back and forth
not knowing why its feet are on the rail
swearing an oath upon a bible and not its honour
looking down into the sea's froth
wishing they were not spiting up to its tired wrinkled face
blood vessels bursting, pulling away after the bell has rung
the boxing match still goes on
tiered against a young opponent
occupied with tens and millions of nowhere ideas
teeth *grinded-ground* into shards and fine powder
let him sniff it, cocaine or sand
both, as long as the Bahamas-headed fast-and-soon plane,
the drug money is laundered and I've lain down again -
have you got the answer?
Is it any better?

This paint is rust proof, this paint is drip proof

it will last a long while
the colour will not go away
it is a choice which is there to stay -
capitalism is -
shot up into pine holed, dark track, veins in my arm
veins in my leg, shot up
long stories, and by the end of it,
we will all be rolling around,
it will be the new phase, the new "pesas"
let me see one last stranger as I still resist, capital city
may it be the merriest greeting between you and me
I will come and it won't be long,
maybe seeing things from an inside look
or maybe a mid-life crisis.

I am surprised to read some success covered literature of a wide, famous, public choice, which turns out to be so fancy, free of deeply second degree fluttering image, clean, unresearched prose, and does not speak of a fantastic story, but mainly or solely consists of paragraph on paragraph of self affirmation, on the worth of our own breath, on the will – o can I? - and of our reject of negative, hateful folk who do not treat us well. The generations of the "I think I can" choo-choo train, riding on, seeking the help of a warm, happy, credible voice, to tell us we are good folks and important beings. Now directly implicated in psychology of small moments and tucking you into your bed.

There's some bombing going on
With a flaming "skol" may we drink the while
the black flag of crossed myself flies before
as picked clean are my resting
lead and sulphur on the freshly burned
there are some B.52s up above
doves of a trench-life's
never forgetful,
the ships sail on, ships
to the coasts with swords and gold
pistols may a single shot
there are somme boardings going on
yo-ho, the universal hymn
oh, how to keep living,
if not hoisting ourselves with
a time to claim
eyes to eyes the *clinc* of cheer
unexpectedly karma in the back alley
I'm on my way and in the wood gallops a deer
who know's where, who know's wheres
bombs are siting in their office chairs
their ways are years from
construction is a game of ever fun,
hemp on one side, on the other, a gun.
A single bullet and a voyage in you
the jolly roger is up your mast,
to live where?
With the diseased and the amputees?
Nah, take it down to the river and push it in
and one day you'll be star *gazin'*
motors rustling in the dark sky

take it down to the river and get some of that' fish
strategically, never again will the alarms' ring
the crowds in the street will on their own run all around
and between flags and tankards
never again fall to the ground,
ruckus

To long a little more and a little longer
angering the giant who will not patient be
with bandages and casts
suffering from being hit with fast rolling, unlawful, speeding timidity
amnesia and fear
who is waiting so near and so carefully
could I ask you a question so you can discover for me
an answer is never so precise as can make you go free
a whiteness of swans hovering with sharp beaks
ricochet of a flat stone
depends on how was thrown
as perhaps the mirror of sky and trees
the blueness has descended
the bluenose coin has tossed to its sails side up
a decision is made to once in a while give in
(never again, and a-never more will -
she is the light-haired, the muse from the Iberians' unknown passed
rabbits are her companions) and climate is varied
as is what makes traveling uncertain
to a thief, a thief,
a thieving knife a long side my ribs
(I think of her, know not what gives
her pictures display more and more
the more I know, the more is there, and present,)
to a little more gets a little older
time flies and crashes over my shoulder and into the vast
to long

Beware the presence which grows more often
to be gentle and a strange blend
a
fictional
more or less
grasp.
Beware the one with the new eyes
she is your friend or is she not
a
rural
dream's eager
envy.
Beware again, the food you spend
gladness at hand is not to rend
a
new language
you speak
to me.

Books of illustrations and so or such
will read some words which still seem much-
; entitled * to be
a
new
warning
for me.

Foremost and after all
doomed from the start is doomed to fall
the arms of the rivers and swamps to call
why once again (the dark clouds of leaves-
here is she with the speeds of life
cheeks as pale as soft and dear
a kiss to thee is an unplanned whiff
the blood of a
where was wake and wonder
his gold was spent with pride
to the Duchess in her misty book)

she is planning against me, an agent of the day
it is the fourteenth of this very month
the days are shorter and come too fast
know not what to do, knows not where to cast,
and off the horse which has carried so far
your feet can dance or can they not
and hold her close her breath is hot
your thoughts aren't clear yet knows
one the same page,
you recognize those
and elude what is distant
foremost and after all
is constant.

Flap jacks, morning flap jacks
running in and out of a crisp
the butter sizzles in the hours brisk
from the cold it has rested
pour it now and watch
charlie on the other line,
calling in to say good day.
The windows opened to light of spring
hours of it have not been long existent
the nice weather is here or a start
the sirup is on the table and butter with
could you ever wish for a finer gift than to serve
and here is something new
see the ways that look at you
they know your name and now your habit
a strange journey for a hobbit,
might just stay for a long time, might stay for a life
to sneak around a hidden elven kingdom and free
a blind speaker will whisper as the wind to me
the curtains in the kitchen smells,
suburban *unrowdy* and calming streets
call it beat, new adventures,
to some drums or down here and there
a generation after a clear cut through the world
let it be (and on the smiling stomach
serving a piece of intensions)

Fluent in the tongue of abstract
the friends with whom I've had the best times
still linger in the everyday smile
the cubist cycles of unholy wars
the ashes of a golden era is the world's normal course
still I miss the music.
Swaying white skirts,
the underground scenes of screams, banjos and distorted guitars
the semi-darkness and semi-conscious
of flimsy temperament and
flames of the forever alone, falling
cliffs of agains the flow, pacifism, communism, and hidden ideas
perhaps if you'd come to class,
if the (open, roughly singing piano
wishing you could hear away from the troubled
,bumping around stepping in the dark with a cigaret
smo)king of the northern lights
trying to be perfect or trying to be alright
come and visit deep fjords and midnight suns
fluently vibrating with the surroundings,
through whole body and mind as a new shape of Schumann's
resonating with your comprehensive eyes
resonating with my mouth and lips,
tip of the tongue as, an iceberg
not seeing this pure sens of *be*
the hull might hit and water seep
sinking to the bottom of where are we
the movements will soon hit the deep.

mother, mother of the whole nation
your whore daughter is on the back seats
your whore daughter is letting herself
mother, mother the laws must pass
they must change and they must evolve
mother, mother, your whore daughter
she is letting herself be touched
everything, and everybody
filthy old men and drug addicts on amphetamines
too broke to buy a prostitute
so surveillance has no brothels
mother, mother, the dangers of night
might see the *upskirt*
touch her thigh
your whore daughter
the sky is a roof under which I dream and sleep
mother, mother, take care of me.

She is on the other line
unreachable hello,
playing hangman
sing the song of recorded sunsets.
Fires in the open panorama,
the look off the distance
all reduced to about more or less nothing
your whore daughter laying on her back
with enflamed breasts touched in their newly ordained size
slowly coming, slow breath
listen to some more and to the rest
mother, mother the line
(has been crossed on and again
over;

may we meet in hopes)
(:says the guardian of golden strings
with wings and things floating on his person-
all-
ity again.
With wings and golden things.)

hello mother of a debauchery and criminal morals
the flowers which blossoms into fruit and the season
cries no, freezes and kills all off.
Mother of a breed as careful
survival is ownership
knowledge is to poses
and the only survival
and adapts quicker
than your disease filled body.

Mother, mother she'd need your help
mother at the brink of suicide
she needs a place to sleep inside
she feels nothing more, at every
a national
and a gesture
a riot in the streets sit-in
beg the better half if there is such
crumbs to fall from a table with empty seats
flagons emptied in a single gulp
briefly floating,
briefly being kissed
briefly naked.

Go to find the right heir
here in this world the thunder,

strings and strands, incendiary fires,
destructive genealogy
capture the image of nature, willing
natures will and aim at random
going against anarchy, going against
theft and at random, doing it in the mud, sick, alley
cigaret butts and *angerly* moaning
your whore daughter
who had not been told anything at all.

Mother, mother, your flag,
waving somewhat of a goodbye
thought to be a patriotic death, across oceans,
across misguided
across me!
Mother, in the end it is with
regrets, same as forcefully pardons
kiss her goodbye,
dressed in red, white and blue
in white and red,
in tidings of hymns
tiered poles with her waving clothes
on her disease-filled body.

I don't drink nothin' no more
and gonna die of thirst out here if
nobody don't do nothin' to prevent this nonsense.
Create some of them lovely blues melodies
up in the air, where tears seem to drop
and corrupt, lying advocates
plead guilty for a gin bottle
ready for these charades to end,
and before the sentence is dropped
have a nice diner, with steak, corn and *fixins*
emptyin' a red wine bottle with (h)a graceful laugh
conjugating verbs to all of the english tenses
smoking a cigar to all of the english tensions
and his honour drops his hammer
tellin' me that I'm a bad man.
And I ain't gonna drink no water
ain't gonna drink no coke, in all the American tradition.
If I come to your house, please, at least admit
holding over a lamp, with a bright orange flame
that for a runaway,
I ain't *doin'* too bad.

You're a lovely person, with having uncoloured haired
angels falling and they are scared
the ground is so close you feel a breath
nipples being kissed
and violins played
you are a lovely person, charming, with a smile
and the rabbits in the tall grass stand on their hind legs
to see this person's bones are broken
a prayer had been sung, on your eyes a token
to cross the river on the boat of a god
stepping onto stones of a different volcano
erupting into dark clouds of rebellion
if I'd have the courage to kiss a little sooner
and say Valentine's comes but once a year
to offer to buy you dinner
I could not, past, into, steer
horns as big as ranges and a ranch
the coyote howls under a cactus branch
filled with drugs of a nature of which, I don't care
they drive through your skin and remove the *beware*
my mind is telling about entropy
and I could never wish to scare you away
dear you're a person who's so lovely
I'd like you so to stay
once I grow courage, your washed out sweater
I will hold in my arms
you're a lovely person

come on, come on, men of a certain breed
get up and cry your need
the brisk adrenaline of victory
satisfaction guaranteed as the old proverbs have spoken
rise through spiritual and accomplished
rise to the sun at the edge of the flat earth
walk straight through the mountains
at their very feat
walk through the oceans without breath
walk out of the door without anger
go to the stars for their council
taste fruit in their right season
walk through the orchards, in their neat rows
as the ships advance, you are no slaves
bark at the intruders
ask why are masters
see fish under the pools and puddles' surfaces
circling in discoloured sunlight
their scales are silver streams
raise your cuffed hands and
walk through the walls
walk to chain gang songs
walk through the temples and climb ancient pyramids
walk every step
walk the mountain side at night fall
your genes and your arms, strengthened and tanned
scared and beaten and smiling
and cowardice holding your empty hand
with timidity at your bedside
with regret in the constellations

excusing yourself, wifely and beaten
scream empowerment and scream yourself
hurricane winds of feelings in marital freedom
sleeves of colours from seeping tea.

gla
ss
es

a mill
it-
ary there
yet?

Pea
-ce
growing

on bloo
-d soaked
soil and blue skies

She is over and elsewhere
and ghostly in my mansion halls
the streets, the cabs, the silent seconds
she is over, and elsewhere, and I still recall.
Candle( )light letters, a gust near the blue
the nights bare cold news from her open new love.
The night is a pair a craving arms
clawing their way to the top of the well
the tunnel of light
my pale, frail skin was damned to dwell
she is over and elsewhere
in honey-dew dreams and covered flowers
countries of beloved escape does not serve
for the banned, the man sent to the woods in exile
bearded solitude and empty stare climbing to heavenly
dreams in the daytime, dullness at night
good luck to stand and good luck to do
she is over and elsewhere
and where am I?
Eating pasta, shirtless, at 3 am
forgetting is maybe soon
hating is a new moon
werewolf instincts to any victim
she is an infectious blood
over and elsewhere
may I awaken and perhaps care that
there is hope.

Common up here with wet *snatchcocks*
abiding serene protocols of drinks and
alcoholic decisions
never
elsewhere
chose a queer way
to the same result.

I am an insane bastard who breaks
shattered glass on old beliefs
could you cry that the times have changed
well suck it up.

*Enters blues bar where the music is loud
the guitars are distorted and singing
slide at the finger
in and out of her
slides on the neck
picks at the strings.

Common up here with new will
with shivs ready for more
details, details, carving pumpkins
festivals, celebrated in shockwaves
with saltpetre treats and lobotomy lottery tokens
special prizes for participation.

Waiting at the bar, waiting so long
I met her elsewhere I had believed
for song long and so sorry
that never had been good in this type of story

the hobo man

I'm a hobo man, oh I'm a hobo man,
singing my hobo tune,
ending some time soon,
I am certain
Lying on my bed, oh-oh lying on my bed
I feel it cold and public
wow, I'm lying on my bed
I'm tired
And I'm confused as hell, I'm confused as hell
cursing my lacked smarts
asylum may be best
but not yet,
I'm a hobo man, wo-ho, I'm a hobo man,
singing my blues
I've got holes in my leather, black leather, tarnished shoes,
I don't feel cold,
I don't feel myself.
I don't feel alive
Empty is my best suit,
I've been wearing for so long
not quite knowing what is wrong
you call me hobo! I say yes that I am!
I don't quite really know,
what else to call me, man.
I'm a hobo man, oh I'm a hobo man,
singing my hobo tune,
ending some time soon,
I am certain.

Something sweet about her all
around the fire on the nights of
a midsummer's eave's plays the
smoke arising away in the dark
I think I've got what's called feelings
demeaning? Strange? Am I a moron or I am deranged?
I will bow to the desires or
a monarch, dressed in stars and silk fabrics
why do I want
and why do we walk solo
I hear a noise and maybe below, below, the ground
about as sweet as is said and is said
about as interesting as all which may be read
and the calls of any formerly known matron
why is she there, who has no passion
has she done nothing but to reject
and here all about all
about lie-ticking wristwatches
try to speak, or to boast, or to charm
more than yourself, it is
give, and do, and give, and listen
and hear a new
time to stop, and hope
and speak as softly
as her voice d'be.

No home to go back to, once again, once more I knew
try and try and you don't understand
your own words and your own hands
towards the right direction
compasses speaking in the right tone
north is the only worthwhile source
the suns meet you as an immobile dial
perhaps the phone will say welcome
perhaps out of another foolishness
rooted and smoked out
- by hunters, by buyers,
by more and more and more
buying and theft and murderers
adored by mass popularity
adored by worship and cult
acclaimed to the presidential throne
confetti, cheers and marching band music
waving peace sign fingers, entering a jet airplane
crooked teeth and clear words smiling
everyone coming to meet
out of the country side, the buildings and the woods
badgers of my race with the locking jaw
asking questions and where to dig
groovy parks and groovy everywhere
let us be
it is hot, life is sweet,
there are seven days in every week
standing naked with greetings abode
lemons are to pick, wherever we are
arms for sale if ever you need two more
white sails from isle to isle

to the fishermen we ask
to the winds we pray
they are the guides who we obey
seasons and shelter, and open skies
thunder away where buzz black flies
man of the swamp surviving is your new hobby
you learn so much, you know nobody
wandering around believing you are crazy
thinking over what has happened
not long ago
a few years without, to know,
hunger so here and gone
without a life to live and where
siting on the side of a path
no thumb up in the air
and you don't know if you care.

In the streets of the city, the trees have died
their branches are still stiff where the smogs still glide
the air is cold, humid and damp,
champion of every other sunset
emptiness, exception to recordings
the laugh-tracks and to modern pop
novels without no other meanings
are a raid with bombs that drop
sleep in my blood and in my blood will mix
rails are a quick and an easy fix
under an assumed name, or under a grave
face with no other choice
with friends whom you run from
with fear in your voice
trembling, not knowing, where and if you are (save
their trees may be cut and may not
would it be clean or would it be
some sort
a premonition
  ,of destiny.

Stop smiling to pretend you are nice
may I ask you why you hate my guts?
In and out of a insulting motion
on the phone to call disgusting
who should I blame but the disrespect, and
the wrongful, non-excuse
thanks for my time or thanks for nothing
thanks to my friends to let me move in,
for the short period of misfortune
hurling hateful speech under by breath
thanking them for letting me nest
and I can't be hungry, cannot dream of much
do not want to bother, not want to intrude
will eat cold cuts, cold acts, cold moods
knowing the right keys to doors
Do I represent the freedom and youth you've never had
am I your dad who beat your mom?
He killed himself, and your story is sad
to avoid further sadness would have been too logical
to think is an abnormal fact
to suicide on a subway railroad track
watch out to whom you lie, and to whom you cuss
do not make such an awful fuss about nothing
stop smiling and stop your hypocrisy
a glass devil through whom I can see
does a barbed wire fence covered with paint
flesh still hanging in fresh cut strips
some called that meat jerky
I'd cut it short for simplicity – to jerk
soon enough the chain will break

the soil, dead, desolate will rake
all will fall
as a cold shower.

Sleeping in a country room, up the hill from the train tracks, where
they are kind and help those they   know.
Sheets I've set up on a small bed, some would think so low, I am
kingly.
Welcome to the life of a traveler,
I welcome in my wide open arms and greet thee.
Weighed down and intimidated by knowledgeable folks
If I haven't been favoured by nature and the best of things,
To tell a great story is an art of life and places
weighed down by an incredible low esteem, and a lack of things
have done
to go to one place and to forget you always need just to have fun
and perhaps to drink
there will be a person to take away the gun
be confident in the alley towards the door
break it down with knocks and rings
one day she might say yes or blues
life will have a different voyage and some other sens
let it work out however it may set itself down, falling from the blos-
somed trees.
The small mattress moves back and forth and squeaks on occasion
who said that it's not good; who said the tea is not warm and the
conversation lively
some women have saved their lives with a thousand and one stories
if you can't find your woman whisk away into discussion
anesthesia by distance, flirt and your very
prison pieces scattered in the air in scent of springs and filthy sex, skin, hair
disperse as it's nice to see your eyes and if you were asked to sit
down, sit down, see down I've said.
Elements of embarrassment and shame of needing, heeded,

affection
never should have given, never will I tell, transform, may I make up
if you have no direction you should always take to the idea of
yourself
seeking, opportunity, seeking opportunity, seeing far into destined
and unlaid
broken and on the ground
piece by piece repossessed
the news will be ignored
maybe returning home, only after I have fulfilled my word, and my
bargain with

Thank you for letting me rest in your bed.
Uncontrolled my hands they roam
I do not know what's in you head
whether approved, wanted or not
waves clash and of sea foam
guns which are loaded with lead
infectious, piercing and bones will mend
I may be blind and cowardly
slapping loss and loss again
yet right now it seems to end
blood red sensitive skin and soft
you take them and place as you wish
being subject to you and lend
as often as needed, at any cost
tenderness in the dark has stitched
warmness under a blanket
warmth of feet, piano of a back
kissing with no timidity
would be lost and running with
passing by and near and swift
clean fear and
learned despair, programmed
giving up looking
closer if you may
there is writing on the wall
do not lack will
reading the graffito
thank you it may claim
for holding on.

In the morning my calling comes
breaking fast with the birds singing in the birth of season
learning in sleepless
you(the doing, and seeking for
decisions have been made,
when we left and when we conceived
when had first breathed
taking off, now, in the morning)

sculpting the final details of here, some living
the mountains around the skyline and raise as cities of men
they brake their eroded forms and they dance in the sun's storms
my beautiful bride of newly explored semitic languages and nahuatl
bazars meets emporiums on the river banks
traders with their necklaces come and show us rituals
pagan altars and deities, herbalism claiming benefice one more
and once
painting on a statue of our new king
a long time since disappeared still marking, and still, may the
benefactor
return with vials full-full of magical and aspirin
one more hammered toss on the chisel
one more nose and an ear, one more detail on the bust
breathes some living thing
walls of caves and galleries
troglodytes of subways and antique economic piggy banks –
music boxes
the final schemes and sketches and details of the Babylonian arts
polishing off these stones and the final

when the student from Paris comes,
sickly from tuberculosis, the breath stinks of rotten foods
a book in his hand in the attic room of addict knowledge
comes together the image of a world
imagine the change which can be brought in the word of either
and each
and action, it is time, and action is time vice versa
when the student from the city comes out
his country suddenly reappears
swallow it like a pill and their unmannerly ways
in the underground train where time is of a grave
importance of winning, importance of having cash,
boutiques open and attract your eyes
they span and sometimes they hide in disguise
and while this language you speak
you may wreak but of library dust
when comes the man from towers and blocs
joy will get from watching his countrymen
roads reappearing to their purpose
when the student from Paris comes,
worldly and shrouded in parted ideas
morals explored and lost of all fears
explains to many who deny their ears
there is a reason
denial is here
you may claim to have no time for such nonsense
when the student from Paris comes
there will be a lot to say

Quit while the interest is starting to fade away)
the greens have grown wild and inaccessible
paths of the nearest lost way
few stones you still can spot
good was for the time you say could be
the hair of locks and lochs of ness
beasts always think can see
reaching the top branch of climbing a dead tree,
(will not come back I dare to say

do not carry the end of my gown,
dragging on the ground
for this is my wedding day and I wish to be alone
who has met him and who has charmed
and who has no stress and cannot be harmed
and who broke a leg without a yelp
clapping tantrum of luck and glass
as toast spoken loud for all to break their bread to
speak no more only for you and me and be back soon
only to lay down once more during one more night
one more bed broken into
a red wine bottle with a cork yanked out and a few glasses
and a spinning room spinning around
because when the dream snaps and snaps a little too clear
the air you breath beginning to fear
don't bother me right now on such a day,
such a moment in an awful manor and such a way
my veil covers my face to keep in mind the *mynd* of
things not thought the whole way through
thunder storms on the ocean stirring grey waves blue
of some attorney papers. Who are we most afraid of
but I walk alone, to be taken, and to take you.

To prove either *prøver* and knighthoods be obliged
look out for what it should and people will allow
obligated to a certain extend
using what we know to join with fellow students
moving towards a greater novel
the great americas in depression and in hunting hope
diving in the waters at the midnight stroke of noon
take a seat please to look towards the moon
pleased to see that from some reality you recognize source
to exploit who we are before we're done running our course
the greatest and best renewable energy of manpower
to prover either *prøver* and step more than in volunteer
the soldier ranked in a line and all quiet with some fear
you've got something to offer and cross eyes, cross
and bitter feelings to the failing of what you see
no. you will, with sharp teeth brotherhoods and
with a drawn sword brother, claims and charlatans stress
hanging gardens of falling feathers, scattered winged
my blood amongst them and each
the drops on the eggshells cracked and
now cooking, or we with flyers and pamphlets and wondering news
democratic petitions, unions marching in the streets
the proof of success is so lonely that it will be proven to you
the proof of success is so large it is measured by whom?
Run and feel good in the new vision of the same
the detail which changes the picture so is the frame
and tries and ties and wears a suit and knocks on doors
thumbs around, kicks a can, says to himself "just one more time"
if it might just be the best offer
how much will cost the laughter of a future day
don't worry it's all been done before the enemy has won a war

and might just bring you down with some simple barter
leave you poor if that they may
and you mop the floors at night in a store
to prove either *prøver* you've tried at least
you've sung the blues at the end of the leash and
in time no regrets, no releases of spells no blame and at least one
the charge to glory was and is a memory for the man
who lies dead of the battlefield a beautiful ride how you felt
you had to be something and had to be
how it all came together
no matter how insane
the way to get there
to stay
that enthusiastic.

- the universe is maybe slowing down(
if vocalists chant
har-
-ä melody
inspired by the fire
sparks dancing in the night of oceanic winds
gusts of waves and camps
passionate stories and speeches given by my friend David
if (there is a sound of stretching ideas and contact all over and all
is over and over the)
globes spinning at random destinations our fingers point
and perhaps with some luck we will export ourselves and loose
the false hopes which still survive and somewhere they
in
a personal record
stab repeatedly
much worse than not seeing the busy streets of a new land
or the sadly less explored corners of a market in which all the
treasures
from the tombs of
(and our fathers claiming the right to the traditional bayonet
that too, you can find and escape and run into again when you've
lost all respect)
running engines, machetes and half communication with mysticism ants
running all   over your
clothes and bag,
stop drop and roll to the fire of beating, breathing, aired open windows
feel your lungs poisoned by lead, half lead, and half a dose of realism,
overbearing,
exhilaration that the universe is maybe slowing down and so simple
in the morning I've loved you, in the evening have fallen asleep
in the afternoon I've loved you and at midday we dined, eyes into

one another
branches and their dried leaves, heaps and heaps we've set on fire
tired of being asked by capitalists and false governments for
advice
that is no way to say "at your service" with a graceful motion,
taking off hats, we are indoors
forty two years later,
soft with fresh fruit and riches felt in our palms and never brought
back but the sent of
the soil,
for the richest thing we've touched with our palms was the bark
of a live sandalwood
                    tree
the leaves of the outgoing outstretched mango and the flowers of
lovely orchids
the perfume of hyacinths floating amongst the walk in an air of
centuries old
(heroes will draw nearer when each of us discovers
that in the "eye to eye" and footed dreams
that -

My soup is cold.
How ever will it get hot again?
With ease I've held smoke
the gods
of modern times
have left me behind in an unfurnished apartment
plumbing and electricity are rare commodities
the very first
unsatisfactory, devout hunger
in the bedroom who is a lover
is the most deprived man
with love for boiling tea
may you want a spoon full of honey
my cigar is lit and a fitted curse upon poor and difficult
housed already complaining
this century, is a century of
satisfying everyman
by unsatisfying the few
the work that she is doing
is work of lords
her heavenly feather blond wings
floating hands of a blind old
lone
deserter.

never used to vanishing
I pray
the deserts are less of a hideout,
padre, without a whisper, bless me
you too are nothing but an entity
giving out to these cacti
a place to fit
and a place to die
a place to dress
and perhaps never really used to vanishing
writing to put down on paper who
we, at the moment, are and are not
too many until for nothing
flames will put an end to our furry
if the cross gives us
the will to be famous
and snowflakes shaking down,
lay'n on the purpose ground
the grass is the company
which also, every season's now and then,
and in the lack of rain and crying thirst
never quite used
bells ringing in the empty streets of town
music to our ears is the prayer of time
taking a little of towns and coasts
never quite used to vanishing

I've drunk new wine
(straight from the bottle
deep in red colour
and lips as fresh)
and I've played with tin soldiers
(with faded paint
without articulations
with imagination in place)
who've stood in a box
(classified and suffocated
by factory and social views
with a mask or a label,
in waiting for a dance)
well dressed in attractive colours
(a poke-a-dot skirt and a white blouse
a stick instead of words
have brought a look onwards)
and I've met a new year
(with different goals and hopes and fears
with a golden touch with what we've learned
it accumulates to get better, and it opens the box)
and have grown older
(through ordinary mail
cards have travelled and I've sent myself
over and over, stamped and trampled
tired and weary,
happy to play with soldiers and their make
happy to lay with some wine,
and to stand around)
see how the glass overflows

(yet not a drop falls
I've bought it cheap,
she is a bundle of joy
and my purpose is with her dialogue, born)
I'd like to see you again
(where are you living? Are you healthy?
Last time we chatted it seemed you were sad
maybe it was one of those days)
who've stood on a shelf
(for no other reason but to sell and to be sold
and to sell themselves to the first passer-by if he can
with a compliment gifted more or less)
to what goal burdened by creation
(to reproduce its same treatment
to have an afternoon of make-believe)
I've drunken wine and played with toys
of a different era.

Running again from something else
thumbing around and living on dirt cheap and songs
from one crop to the other and one another backache
without problems with the law but the state a problem
with a family we still know but have not seen in long so
unclean half the time, on the way there the rest
if there's one place that's a direction it's for no god damn reason
and if there's one star shining in good fortune over his head it's
out of pity
sewing his torn shirts and they get torn in the state of Maine
they get torn in Canada and in San Diego
they get torn in debates, street fights and nights of sleep
restless sleep in full dress and nights in which you passed out
nights of shadows and nights of wide eyed excitation
good times in Berlin and in Las Vegas, Nevada
if you can name a place any more useless on the face of the earth
I'll give you a prize
                maybe it's just why I like it
        perhaps you'll even call it home when you're tired and alone
        when you've used up every other option, when you're lost
        call it home like you call a woman beautiful
        call it a different name and it's all the same without the beer
goggles
        impatient to get back to wherever you were before
        dreaming of where you've never been
        running away in every direction, hands are in the living dead
                his Majesty calls upon the humble man
here is another morning feeling empty and cold
here is another morning waiting for the sun
itself is being chased or being pulled up
being picked up by your shirt collar, yelled in your face

"yes sergeant" you reply before squeezing one on the crapper
being forcefully fed your meals
do not worry, you are protected, under a cannon, under a bridge
where can the power not be left to its own candle lit dinner
when I came by her, softly whispering – the world awakens
from anything at all really, anything that's been laying
covered in dust and in unwanted memories and *pleases* and
thank-yous
getting a lift to whatever's the next town and the next station
wherever solitude can be and will the solution to find.

You know you are "not" under a dictatorship when small towns
own tanks
where arguments are of protection and crisis situation response
and once there will be cause for revolt
to the volts of electroshock
the bullets your bodies, the crowd will rock,
and waves of cheer with an arm straight upwards
and their armoured hulls won't be affected by stones, by Molotov
cocktails
when cougars will pounce on outraged proletariat workers
ecological conservatism, protection, a threat to the ambitious and
oil fuelled
        governments
and the cops have more budget than artists and the community
projects they protect
the army is richer than the people they protect
we will be saying "thank you mister officer man"
sitting in my chair still wondering why the hell who elected who
is it patriotic to dumb down your senses
and not to fear the weaponry they prepare
"do not wonder about this missile, which is pointed at your house"
morality and consciousness
to blindly trust the ones who can be corrupt
in bed with whoever can be
a rough and infected sex addict
giving the impression that they are all the same
there is no medicine, do forget their trade
the plants with pesticides are <u>spayed</u>
herb-witch standing over my bedside as I throw up
claustrophobic and scared
saddle up and yell a Lotna's charge
with courage if and for,
as long as we are not under a dictatorship.

pardoned by meeting conspirators
pardoned by breaking rocks
and still, stale make-belief
that fluttered looks been less than brief
looking into the motion of kissing you
pardoned by governments away in their
vanity and vain to the logical discussed
pragmatic envy and nature and hormonal
and the body of another
step up to the call and the draft
tonight every theatre will play
shooting the silver screen in practice
salute of the soviets, farewell from the mob
meeting none other to comfort weeping away
to claim the same of the bag and the sob
tonight, every theatre will play
when thoughts away will of four scores
pardoned by motion.

I who am forgotten by your clocks
behind your known moves to live in a box
who is late and who cries not
sits in front of the lot
in a crow's nest eggs and snakes
up, up at the top of the mast
casting wet spells
which fall down, and are raked by your street cleaners
foretold by law and logic of bare acquaintance
have then been crooks or simply not clever
and the tranquil travel now hunted, by circumstances
in iron cages, or of cement and passing all
plunged and purged in rain, ponds' frozen water
through green burned red light-orange the flame will save his filthy soul
who may try to once again come together
figuring out the concept of how long and short they chase each other
in our age came digital for all to capture simply
and between troubles what is to do?
Patience my son, with courage your virtue
casting wet spells on paper scrolls
tire not a morning strolls at once carrying the sun
down the boulevard with my hand out for the warmth
tinders of the golden rays on my pale skin
tinders of the golden rays on rooftops
the newspapers under my clothes mention the president

will you come to me, in the morning light
will you come to me, in the morning light,
my lips will whisper
when the time is right.
When the hours are of electric light
come have diner with me without prior planing
out of decisions just like the wind
good-day in our sails are storms ahead
adventurous making out maps on the couch
of whom I will know every nook and cranny
to drive past without waving
in the morning light, when you come to me
my lips will whisper
when the time is right.

Tremble til the saturated clouds
Saturn related to the rest
the star guides my shepherd's herd
scales of the slimy moon
eagle's sights passing by me
quick she is the enemy
faster than the days
worshiped and sacrificed again
hear the lord and lady
emptying the last drops
the number is written with a pen
boil the water and seep the tea
will you come to me in the morning light?

How I want to see them
walking the midnight path
the deserted roads and in total twilight
hailing every step, wanderers
gambling with betterment,
peels revealing a rotten fruit
suddenly the leaves sway as oceanic music
walk through the rows
pick the juice and bite
softly,
my lips will whisper,
when the time is right.

Stowaway once more may I stay unnoticed
by language may I travel a yokel or a tourist
every means through woods of topmost hills
stowaway in my shoes until the time stills
eating all sorts of strange things forgotten in my pack
do not want to speak, and be left in my tattered clothes
had too much to drink and lone will sit feeling morose
watch me not friends who'd have pity
as much is hard to hold in sorrow of my sorry
controllers have not yet crossed
A newly chosen stop
stowaway where there's not as much security
and confident outgoing the world is yours
knowledge and meaning drinks every pours
frightened tears empty of arms the splashing on the ground
spirits from the grave tear clothes, skin and have, me, found
could they shut up with their unhappy rants
their bickering leading to none
words bouncing to judgemental silence
Idiots,
building upon more frustrations and
goodday I'll take my bag and leave
with respect for my tired bones
none to complain my misery
happy as all who talk too much
taking further, heaths to heart
in a corner if is to mean regret
every which way leads to standing back up
no wine our _whineless_ breath and red smiling stained
baggages in the wagon of stowaways

centred around your own linted belly button
of passed juvenile sexual theories
conceived in nationalism of a third type

1ˢᵗ nationalism:
       a glorification of the nation within the rest of the world,
accepting differences   and similarities, keeping them in
mind and knowing who we are and respecting others in this
regard.
Tends to bring openness of mind, social and philosophical ad-
vancement and good international relations.

2ⁿᵈ nationalism:
       a conservative radicalism glorifying the nation claiming its
superiority above   the rest of the world and imposing its ways
to eradicate inferior ways.
Tends to bring xenophobia and other sorts of closed minds raging
wars for some reasons, on somewhere with undesired ways.

3ʳᵈ nationalism:
       an ignorance. Glorifying your nation without know it, because
you do not know   anything about the world beyond. Imposing
its ways because you do not see the necessity, the use, the
purpose of another way of doing.
Tends to make idiots.

Born in a cabbage or born in a rose
children growing in their native plants
for a stem to pop out of the garden's perimeter
will be pulled or mowed and tossed away
the grass is greener and fertilized by bullshit

we are the best nation by our statistic
to declare myself the saviour of man,
everyone surviving, speaking, living
testimony of contradicting truth
the guns will go off when there is nothing more to say
when there is nothing more to add
let's not forget the nationalism of colonies
let's not forget the debates around the rights of humanity
blacks are people, women are people, children are people
nationality is not you, you are not subject
man is free
the world is a series of exiles

At least they won't call me out
step to the line of bayonetted guns and a single bullet's
unknown soldier with a uniform, any uniform,
random and a stranger in your own nation
regional expressions of the same language
standardization and an exploiting class
how do we choose if not out of an ass
when or where they will call me out,
negro of my interior skin.

I've been everywhere and driven to empathy
you are human and do not like to loose
maturing, learn to listen to reason and grow with consensus
and opinions are a pivoting platform on a table
orders are filled and are shared and lively
happy birthday it's where you are
Age is nothing like death.

At least they won't kick me out
with uniforms of border-guarding muscle
with their crossed arms, crossed looks, crossed thoughts
if even
"and get out, and get away",
you will hear from everyone
how has stayed, at home, at school,
and who dreams of home, and of school,
aimed by a bullet and its row,
prison
an
unknown war.

When you are seventy and full of wisdom we may talk
you will see things through the eyes of meditations
by I who am younger than you.

Where have you been and what have you seen?
To order around your opinionated stubbornness,
thought the whole thing through
and been bothered by what?

Can we talk without insults, my friend the citizen
your definitions have not yet suffered
you stand and yell for your concerns
perhaps have you benefited from solidarity,
you have not shared.

In the near future, my aging colleague,
trembling and tired, too late realize,
there is no need to be scared.

Colleges may earn you knowledge
where will intelligence flourish
critiquing and interpretation
is the progress we seek.

One day in tolerance and comfort with yourself
and a prayer in your temple,
heaven awaits an upwards stare,
wind raking the farm of clouds
dreams and sails and
wider horizons
which aren't you.

Welcome
to the new diet, to the new words
to the new plants of the new worlds
to the new books and the new techniques
to heliocentricity.

Welcome my friends of conservative ways,
to eat fried worms here for the next few days
to leave for India tomorrow morning
and milk the Kamadhenu without drooling.

Welcome to where you've never been
where you will be humble
where you will not bother and be bothered
and discover and know, the meaning
that you are small.

Troubles soon to be over,
in Judaic golem protection —
rise and buy me a living
near Karl Marx and near myself
no aspirins and no water
no more jumped train connections
hours which are so tiering
and lay burdens on floor and shelf
no more, I said no more crying to the river,
no more weakly apologizing
inadequacy crowing at the only bleak light
in a rut without interruption
shingles falling off the day after day roof
day after day with winds and rainstorms
the door creaks and paint chips
fool of a man following his inherited envies -
learning and making something of your *unscorched* hands
, a man without land is no man at all,
and I can't be satisfied until at once and suddenly
here there is a phone call or a letter arrives
and reading in the ink
happy tears watering flower blooming eyes
colour of the morning and the smell of fresh bread
around the hour is the bettering of today

I'm one good family away from being out on the streets
I'm one friend away from giving up
I've never learned these things and am confused as hell
to which paper to fill and in which bureau to yell
or to be supposed to wait, outside, in the cold
for someone to gently hand us a sandwich
an earl might somehow want to make something out of us
stagnant in a puddle pond of impermeable ground
how will you end up being fifty?
To be rich, to have a family at home, or to live in a windmill
celebrating your birthday with your roommate, a twenty year old
communist poet
the flapping of wings as around you they move up
and the broken bone, crooked and pain
might just pick at the seeds on the ground
staring at the branches on which nests are built
in their foundations of jumping down on your own
stay calm and cast a gris-gris talisman in stone and cloth
say it again, say it, that it's nobody's fault
look at the military airplane which flies above the homeless
sturdy, stand up and vote by raising your hand
respect for opposition is as important as knowing every fact
push the button, do it in self destruction
vote for no one you would not abandon,
a deserter in a bad mood

you sent us to get killed and for the generals to stand behind tables
some have their reasons – where is another Zhukov? –
from out of the garbage and the sewers I come out with red
burning
and a gaze of liquid through the fissured walls
when the establishment crumbles(.) and their offices
may they see where I am right now with we
and building state from the ground up
with the mother, father, the children, the uncles and aunts
helping each other with their individual paths
in, and away

This morning I woke <u>myself</u> up
no cereals to eat and not to go somewhere
rabid smoke coming out of ears
as I clutch a nearby beer bottle
speculating angry words as withdrawal
up and at them, it will take no time

some morning myself would be a rosy moan
of the buzzing bees pollinating in
the summer petals after the rain
when the swans flap their wings,
gently gliding on the green coloured river,
moss on the trees before their leaves, us, cover
in shade and in laze of romantic afternoons
of mid-century bourgeoisie in its richest form;
the one without things, without items
when we have not we invent what we own,
nothing more than the clothes and our hats,
a look we have and hone
inverted daydreams of my awaking eyes
a visage as a desert, thirty mirage and *wolte*
and a rosy cheek as I kiss you groan
fantasies from an underbelly drunkard to love
never again clutching sadly
no one and waking *myself* up to see
nothing in the glazed look of tasks
of shallow magazine articles
of picture perfect edited skin
no one will guess and who will win?
In absolute beauty
dollhouses; who does not wish

to go back and play so
and we invent bureaucratic tasks once and once more
one at a time and here is a job
I dreamt yesterday that things were
at their full potential of freedom
and free making
and substantial living
money in a bank just siting
where and to what goal is a monetary system,
which benefits no one
if we were born not for social improvement
and our bodies do not adapt
this morning I woke myself up,
shaking me, with my hands on my shoulders
saying "get up, the sun is shining"
a bad schoolchild I flung my wrists to away me
back to sleep though, when to will it how?
I cannot get back to dreaming now,
with clouds being blown off again
in the shapes of their randomized follies
when drops will rhythmically puncture my window
I will be under their bound and wishful
freshness like wind and so
to breath more than your own dust
during the storms, shutters flapping and
stained glass is the image of the greener side

Some morning, myself fooling with feelings
sentimental issues and the crash of a day on the rise
to motivate to stand up and to take
your spoonful of sugar
and I thought I communicated with
once again and once more, man,

could you hurry up and make haste
there are kilometres to walk
magic ships to which I hold up my thumb or bite
and we wonder, I wonder, the rain might come
need to get around, the clouds are hung,
the roofs are low, jumping one to the other
they hear underneath me the sound of pitter patter
they hope for Santa Clause
they see nothing but a dropout, draw back
drawn back to strange roots,
called by conscience, loss, lack of consciousness
tortured by thirst of what we are too shy to ask
standing in front of the showcasing window of the street accessed
stores
unaccountable for awkward silences and silenced by uncertainty
your interests and your personality
trying to be polite and unaccountable
going someplace nice and showing
that it is possible, and even unbalanced,
crazy and unstable motherfuckers
can be nice people.

Offering to be up early with the rooster's crow and the
red eyes glowing as if drugs, shooters and pills
and smoke all in my nose may cough
I may get ill from tired dizziness
still rise til and stand with a flag
and with bags under shutting lids
and submarines, invisible radios
look forward, unique and scarce of blood
people sucking on every one of your coloured veins
in pouring liquor
let me be drunk and take my morning offers

if I have my beer in the street do not moralize,
I am the son of a beat society
and yards of satin have flown over my head
I am unfolding the breath the sun just kissed
away
as this morning I woke <u>myself</u> up
shaking around head and exorcism
folk music of thyme and apples
community dances do not raise themselves
out of fear to ask for her hand behind our tie and neatly combed
hair
where you going with that luck in your hand?
I know exactly because I have a plan,
in the meantime it all starts right now
this morning as I wake myself up.

Goodness to the willing
accomplished be it so
to the sighted of nameless life
renaissance shall then grow

Goodness to their strength
numbers can it see
the countryside of every land
perhaps is part of "me"

Solemnly swear to lords who have
names engraved and all
their whips crack on folks
who without they might fall

The willing and their peace of mind
laze in the resourceful starving
to the helpful comes respect
in return in times need saving

Greatness to the unnamed
sagas of golden cities
citadels of the hammer's wielder
and freedom to the possessed claims.

I pissed in her shampoo to see how clean she gets.
I might have an empty head and a rotting brain but I still know
how to get revenge.
Sometimes I zone out and think about evil things
where I am and the crystal clear
honey will soon enough turn to solid
do not ask for divorce honey, let's do this like mature individuals
I don't like sleep and having to eat,
I don't like what a few months have done
ship your package, the goats are kidding
with their gentle smiles and human screams
winos whom, I can, with, collaborate
they all watch the same television programs
and when they go to the can they all do the same thing
easy to microwave and an easy bowl
siting confused with a tired hood the pause button is now dead
and forget about it,
while comfort somewhere else, is the only comfort you will get
for the while
bubbles are better than nothing

in the docks' early hours
with the foghorns in dim light
the house has shown the path before
remember me in spite
schizophrenic moved, eventful past dusk
the orange twilight of town
where people and their glowing eyes
squint if they are not alone
and if their path is hinted with
aromatic oils of incense sticks
moaning in the evaporated drapes
curtains of the churches of coastal fairs
and turbulent dirty sailors
crates hoisted by ropes and delivered
all taken again elsewhere
please be kind
there isn't loads of time
maybe a chanty, a beer and a brothel,
it's not possible *otherways*
it's not possible to stay, once more,
with a cold and mixed
frowned morning
frowned daybreak
there is no other way
to buy
your ticket
take your seat
one side meets
the life of a daily type.

I'm walking along this road
walking under the sun
and the wind is blowing cold
and I'm waiting for the day to be done.
So that I can sleep, and I can hope that I won't wake up in pain
that muscles will relax and joints won't be stiff
win trust, win signatures
and courtly manners wearing
white suits of everyday use without aprons
how hands can stretch it
how big can your man-arms carry
I'd like to drink some tea
spoonfuls, spoonfuls,
beechwood, sawdust
clothes are fluttering in their clouds of rust
weather is of little importance
to cool down or to keep dry
sweat allowed to disobey
can they be blinded by the day
or the umbrellas they call hats
raging their whips on the nights of witches
on the eyes in the dark
and on the nine times lived
blowing horns
down gullies the technique is based
and we don't have to pay what we have not baked
in long and hand-rolled
these are not cigarets
jazz cats putting down the
after a toasty jam – pass the butter
dripping onto asphalt

and the whipping whispers of leathered wind
and somewhere there will be a place to lie
if they are not writing it down
I can hope to sign a lease.

Fried by loneliness my brain is tired
and the burnt toast my knife is scraping I've lost interest
live as it goes on in a direction of known structure is strange
and perhaps if every morning would be different
gladly with travel will change
vacation is an empty mess because outside of work I do... what?
Can I escape troubles alone with bare palms
it the trees under Mediterranean sun
perhaps I would drink and go a bit wild
and the shell would shatter
I am no one but a stranger.

Softly whispering while sleep
sunglasses and Cadillac hair
scared and putrified
time goes by so fast and we learn slowly
and to do what we ever will is an estranged story
and to get up is a bothersome chore
when the sun dies out and the injection comes
before the electric chair, a burger and servings of fries
be generous before the crying game of disease
brain dies sooner, or as this break comes apart
the vacation of an early spring
sinful in our last days of work
with a smile and something glad
may I bury my lost nerves and craze fidgeting eyes
back where I can understand
my temporary purpose.

Burn the witch, oh burn the witch!
Who gave the illusions and trouble
crops have failed
conclusion
her prayers to the devil bring his will
the stores have costs raised to more
spells of want and costs what for
a product brought for the soul of who knows
in banks away the profit goes
burn the witch and CEOs
who've brought the illusions and trouble.

hermit from between the dunes who leaves footprints in the sand,
to end up wherever he is, tired and can barely stand,
to think back wherever he had once been joyful,
and still runs towards that feeling knowing it lingers around here
because it   doesn't evaporate for the sun beaten ground,
and breathes under the concrete, all though it is hard.

Some people are nice in the world
they gave me a lift
(to where I'm going
I will get there smiling)
Nothing heard the chirping top branches
swaying in the old poetry
in switch liquor the *veynes* of earthly history
the roots they dig and tell us to stop by
there was a day without telephones
and never call the ones who, on adventures
would loose each other for only a moment
the gay walls of existing uncertainty
lead your fate into a cloudy space
observe the telepathic evolution
never will it leave the *upways* thumb
the visit on a Sunday afternoon
saying good'ay to roses and dear old Ms.Duboise
as she thinks in her time
is the worth of a quarter and a dime
digging the garden of a back ached gardener
where are the flowers this year?
Where are the bees?
Honey, could you hand me the jar
breakfast is ready, and I would like to
serve it in bead, the news papers
look a little more lively
some people are nice
as I helped, look at what he gave me
is a smile
time to depart! Time to leave!
The horn is already ringing

the engines are on the run
there is a lot to see out there
and with welcoming arms
we have always co-existed
is ethnicity our thoughts
a part of the village is a part that
never will there be another community
like the one of childhood

with a nostalgic eye on the calm of social
and lightly before and could ignore but a whole hoard
aggressive and rushed, speed head with coke
sit down with the generals who rage war, who have a smoke
and joke about such matters to keep people busy
they're doing us a favour aren't they?
Well with an economical base let me see and treat
at bay inspired foes, the Shaolin spade as versatile
digging, and proceed to my martial arts
to the courts to solve problems which may be so simple
as to look deeper into the dried river bed
silk fabric and that is golden, man, I like it,
you go where you must be to open up your thoughts

Spank me harder! Oh, spank me harder!
I've rented this room
not for any more days
as long as I stay here
I will see how people live.

Spank me, with the different
I've rented this room
to find which keys
spank me as I lay lain down on your knees
crying chicken broth
for the masochistic soul
the paper airplane
open wide here it comes
messages and flying high,
on wordplay let me feel good
cheer up even the latest
studios are empty. The streets are cold
to a blood red, to a skinny
wigs and artefacts of red lights' Amsterdam
I would like to hide nothing
worth a damn
speaking out loud about pederasty
and Mexican fantasies,
mistresses with a horse included,
Brazilian nights with barely dressed
assaulted sexual diaries
emptied wallets and mixed feelings
do not dare once more
to conceal a reputable escort
Mr. politician with a briefcase

carrying the heads of every whore
giving him their heads
giving him head-s
whatever is on the top of the table
what you do not see
is it manly in football
is it a joke
spank me harder for all who boast

spank me harder dear!
Bating for the championship leagues
basses are long behind yet we still must
and make me scream, wield
the hammer on the metal
the pen with the ink
the quill is sharpened
wave it home
muttering black slang
sealed and stamped
trampled old hobo
call you a nymphomaniac without opportunities
I'll spank you see what'cha gonna do
and see how the power
and I say power,
I say *Wazzap* with stress at the end
sticking out your tongue
dirty parrots
brigands and mercenaries
believing in stills
let's table this meeting
table your knees
how was it last night
when the alarm clock still rang

are you the night guard
who sits with his cup in hand
watches the streets
where real wacko's roam
flat palm and aggressively horny
oh spank me, oh spank me baby

they've all crossed our path at least this once
when the rent is payed all town is groovy
with highs and lows the music is playing
do not scratch it if you want to dance.
Tune up to Harlem and breath easy
bags are full of books, what else would it be
can we talk about
going worn south
where the living should be easy
crosse the border
felon with hooves a stomp
to the sunset the hot air
come on and build
where you have found
and, or, elected,
home
where no eyes are in the bedroom.

New hope is in the air *muddafucka*!
New life is in my bones!
I have a rendezvous in the evening
never have I joyed more moans
smile at me and smile at you,
tones were nice and words were too
let me sign with wallow Mr. President
our boys' lives are at this present
molasses cookies in their hands!
New sparks in dim
they were lazy and falling forward
may I go through this week once more
to rise like that, once more, once more,
can you feel the wide swinging open door
hearing the high pitch squeal of an antiquity,
with a fire pit and localities,
sens the heat and steam and hunger sore
search has ended or continues, once more, once more,
you mother' with a vicious chain
stick it to the taboo-ed incestuous or into my wheels
anesthesia!
OK ultra whilst the rest of the world will snore
here to keep here to keep here to keep
awakened thoughts and anxieties until here is
to satisfy for at least the next good news
hope is in the air you motherfucker
skin wears as a suit
bowties as wings they flutter
the butterflies of a nightly chic

in the night of blossom
spring has finally bloomed
leaves under moonlight lamps
and shapes emerge out of captivating rites
raising their naked bodies near the windowsills
the daisies have raised before the forms
which in the decline
will lay filled out
in piles and piles
on the foreground
fairs with wheels of skies
take us near reaches of atmosphere
where noon is closer
and is not yet quite so near
as the pollution of every streets' safety
rapists in the deepest reared country
make me believe an aurora
radiation of patience or of quick sunburn
they may put up solar street lamps in those nordic countries
turbulent night, turbulent and trying
not to flood the coastal regions,
not to eat the parcels of land
the portraits of dunes
limited to their height and randomized shape
bring me to survival
lead me the *Sinagua* way
see how abandoned
turbulent times of night when we run in our horizontal sleep
yelling though nets of drool
sorry we missed you
if your petals were having nightmares too

under the oil moon
under the lights' lamps and the ways erased
the myths now prance and the revolts raise green flags
and Tripoli has fallen to stay behind
soil growing between our fingers looking down
looking over red rocky mountains of Alberta
where do we continuously fish two headed newborns
ai, ai, ai, how winter is bad
how we can sens the size and dimension
and how much time it takes to walk a mile
grown up, legs so tall and steps long
and over corpses, fissures and earth quakes
how we can sens the rainforests
tidings of undead cultures
villages without disruption,
with fruit forever
without airplanes
without petrol
with meat from their hunts
with fruit forever
Icelandic underground, quickly take cover
in the midst of this northern night
have baskets been filled
drilling in a fermentation process
prose of modernity
soon enough will be a business
do not cry down near the roots
stare up to where buds and bees
failing to warn
March twenty-first.

I miss attraction, initial breathlessness and holding the hand of a stranger. We have barely talked yet we would do more than a lot for each other, and already, as if a bridge in our brief conversation, have your shoulders been constellations, abstract and smooth of edges. Have we pulled away from the crowd to smooch without speaking intentions and intending knowing ourselves what's up. I would like to be firm and hold you, and I miss noticing a wonderful lady, and through luck of somehow, reflect on the past in the near future, barely to believe that it has happened, that it was possible. I miss having subconscious body language speaking in my place,

good day Lucifer
can I get a proposal
can you ask me for something
and I'll answer with a gamble

good day Lucifer
climbing up right ladders
good day Lucifer
stand on top of those stars n' sky

I met the devil at the middle of a bridge
trees hanging over the waters as newly dead's widows
can you correct my delinquently misunderstood
characters we play to be who we may want to
inhabit it, and accept
a *should* is as immortal as it all will start again
as shoulders will turn leaving and beheading
and in a basket, handed, and perceive, for a mirror
a frown is sewn with black thread
dreadful grip on a scalp, or sickly, upside,
stuck in your throat
to turn it the other way
to seem to be okay

good day Lucifer
can a get a good deal
I won't keep it very long
but could it have some appeal

good day Lucifer
making worth while time
good day Lucifer
take what had always been mine

compasses clouding night shifts
masts where the winds lead our drifts
sextants where st. Elmo's fires shimmer
the boreal's sheets drape the way
milk is the mirror on which we sway

let it be til there is no more sea
burn their rumours that have been spread
we are merchants and bear no dread
not all of us doors the same key
and we will wear your signs to buy our bread

until romantics bleed a nation
the way northern in each and all's
as it had been in the union
no more for now the spruces
keep tight the seeds in case
once more the earth will be covered
scaled with dragons' heads
crossed flags and contested tongues
blown around the gusts of coasts and Baltics' lake
imagined not as of late, will

some they have, they give, they want they
could it be therefore me
all there is, the prancing, dancing, juggling
coins, you clown with red your nose
hairs out nostrils of thunderclouds
bolts of zeus' drawings on pots
smoking torches and pitchforks
of peasant *revoltings* for many a thing
in your pockets they dance as rockets ranging for war
aiming themselves to the ones they adore and again
some they have some want to give
should it be the right and wins
hooray I claim there are no names
on dead we found, therefore no claims
oh how we like dead with no names
no sad families, no widows
calm yourself, breathe through your nose
sometimes you would need a nanny
to tuck you in and call you dear
do not stress oh so small man
soon enough there, in a face down position
rebaptized a stone in a park
a resting place for arms which have so long reached upwards
can you believe this!
Nonsensical losses in the very same way
accidents happen every day
some they give, they want, they speculate
how to own more of this a murderer
controlling the lives and how they crash
how is consciousness of a boss of a large array
tentacle gripping handles if it may and if not

get lost you! Get lost and hunt and gather
try to climb up a different ladder and barking
up another tree they hear
barking, yapping, dogs and words
to chase the mail or to yell at birds
to chose, to lose, to be once more
the masses stomping about and ignoring
the lightness, the thinness, of ice bear's clubs
the seals are best not either
do not jump to make it thinner
and push the rooms with crowns and staves
which might just yet but performed
songful and with illusions of Mao's will
somewhat want
and success
that some they could not have.

Something of a spare second was enough to hear the voice
I've been wearing this hat against the sun
spring has finally come as it does one day
not any different than any other beat' spirit
it was enough to get dressed and get out
and hear a slight silence
play those strings if it don't make no sense
if it doesn't or if you have to dig and look harder
in the air of a different month
in something of a split and a splinter in your hurting thumb
hold it up if you agree, push it down if you build
and is it because I enjoy tradition and culture that I have to be
closed off
and to keep it with the ever changing and effervescent future
and the cattle trampling through
every wrong direction or a severed limb
if I'm ok that I have won
if I don't go no place then I can't win
and in the split opinions of my compadres
never commenting the same book
accommodation and in something of a second
open shirts so as to cool off
there was a salvation
for all

It was a bad vibe all of a sudden
you can ignore Spartacus at your knock
down crying and wonder
where will you look
and the midnight proper walks
light the matches that,
in their eager greed
shall respond to light.

Pull out every arsenal,
eager cannons stuffed with powder
the faces whitened
the pages which no longer mean anything
the faces whitened
will they bleed under amnesic plaster?

It was uncomfortable
when they walked in with their reason
with reserved or eventual seats
and progressive state,
at the balcony or the terrace
it was as strange as Russian roulette
which once was a pastime.

After, I imagined a little more
remedies
for however
your skin
is so soft.

(I know, my silence has been detected
talking is no use where the eyes have winked)
they call me an ancestor
skeletons chuckling in the wind
as light wears its elbow-length gloves
sweetly tripping
as drips down your light haired figurine
of porcelain and flasks or tinted glass bottles
for;

Remedies,
however
a little more
does your skin seem soft.

The largest lakes and the tallest mountains
and the mist of their twilight hiss
burning witch hunt and envy of steaming
cottages where all grows
to do what the tongues told
to walk through the woods without light
of a waxing moon filtered through the
mares of hungry treetops
where they chase tails down trails for the fun of howls
reaching at once I do not kiss

remedies,
however
your skin ever more
smells sweeter than to touch.

Stone houses with no heat
to stop the wind from the sea
to have no fires but to mix
Remedies,
to however
your skin
is so soft.

Delayed
and left to the waterfalls
composite postcards
briefs' details
and they echo through the terminal.

Gates moved
to some crescent pearls
remained siting
in the shape of the lotus
and they echo nearing the terminal.

A pass in hand,
a seat for a moment
and when they land
to recognize
real once again
never again will reappear
as they echo through the whispers
of the instants
of the terminal day.

Sidewalk dirty bastard
hands in his pockets and in his turn
fantasizes about his good friends
holds down his boners with envy
and too shy to revolt
spits on the cement.

Sidewalk so grim and despaired
with the amounts of drugs and cigarets
tossed its way and stomped in
do understand what it means
to pile up junk
for the yard is a whole other atmosphere
and do not be the dullest of the un-showered
have a drink of water in a tall glass
add ice cubes, add a squirt of lemon
quench thy thirst
in the hot shade
of after-hours.

Do not believe people want something else than you
that specialty in the mirror you see
and that envy as held back
should be released
onto the lips
of the costumed
accustomed.

O celebration,
champagne and all
bubbling on
sun burnt crisp of caramel skin
rippled thoughts
thinking lines
forehead
inventing new guides
and chanting on
their new coming
in a feast we crowned the king
walking forward
oh happy day
we graduate
and run away
in forward strides
to stand our eyes glancing
and a dare to truth
to be our youth
in treachery and success
corruption will do you best
if you do not look forward
and look as snappy
your comeback may come in handy
neck ties, bows and butterflies
on the tracks or right besides
there is no harm
can do you now
to jump the passing
paying for closed lids
and feed your skin tight

to be better cooked
than in the can
where labelled
some better brand
where the smoke rises
to
celebration.

I am the one who sits under( )ground
who lives, and who knits and who can never be found
swamps abound as mosquitoes dance
smacking the blood onto my burnt skin
the craftsman of metals
veins through the stead
hammered down when made to glow red
the wind blows to such machinery depts
changing us to dwarves of the old
worms squirming in the rot of the mold
soldering rails linked in a hiss
abyssal corrosion, cores and breathing urbanism
running the streams on the unclean walls
anesthesia of standards fore a learned despair
will all retreat, when time will need, to my lair, to my lair.

They have banged with that hammer and they have banged
if the fences are not up, then too long
have the bulls died on such pastures
for their mallet has banged all day and night
planks are nailed and we might freeze to death
so pass on the bottle so I'll forget that I'm to perish.
My head is aching and I can snap at any second
I feel so tense I should lay down
leave me alone so I can cool down
or I will have to go
for a very long time
in the footprints of so many lost men.
Their arms must be so tired,
could they not sit and dine?
They have banged their hammers on nails and wood planks
for what good? Draw it out in song
maybe if they would hunt they'd eat
they would not ask for more.
Sleep under a skin that you've made your own
live in a body you feel.
If the land is sick you walk along with it
and start making a prayer fore every meal.

You know where they hid the stash and you said nothing
the worms can licks your breathless cheeks and
if you get lucky
we can escape together
and make it to someplace
we will care nothing about
with a whole heap, that we will have found
in the stash, which you know where it is hidden
and you said nothing.

If a man dies, do you have more freedom?
Don't you say there is no more right
no more wrong
where do you walk,
furrows a graveyard of miles
saying the earth is dry,
trying to grow crap where you can't even have a decent well,
don't you ride no more
with self righteous, easy,
redemption speeches
gone judging the folks down yonder
who ain't any less of sinners
than the one who claims air for himself
and rages war for a crown upon a head;
let me tell you,
there ain't nothin'
but independence
in this world
or in the only.

Whether or not the withered weather will wear the crowning thoughts of thee
through the gloom which wraps forever no warrior has been taught to flee
on which end of spear or sword will the chosen destined be?
Throw the crown into the pond and see if the frogs they fight
if they lead a wayward bounce that may be for they caught a fright
the splash arises as mushrooms' blaze; clouds across the skies with light
where shall run the therein folk whose scattered feathers fly?
It was not in their own favour that was blinded a left eye
who thought and sought to find best elsewhere, and so has said goodbye
subject once and subject again
where is law to save all men?
To kneel down an oath in favour
that we know they shall live better
hoping the storms aways will blow through the lands are grazed
by sharp and strong and worms of doubt which have not praised
but have worn the skin, and walked within the chambers of velvet floors
which have decided and stabbed so often the cattle in our moors
stand on a lookout with eyes peeled and shout, if they curse haith
on which end will grasp or be taken in all sands of pilgrims' faith
who will learn the books enlightened, who will not be wraith?
Wrath and rather kill in defence than let them run again free
toss it all and see what happens, places to fill still will have a key

coming nearer to the tearing origins
the skies are clear, hugging the open
and the repeating
clouds
of standing
urbanism.
Where climate could believe
that the drift in similar
channelled
ways.
Scraping on backs of mountains
made to transcript
better ready the stance
of new
and explicit circulation.
Highways
delight my ever growing distance
if the lanes are useful
ripping apart
scars drying
on the blind eye
you wear a hat.

Thievery comes unexpectedly
as a shapeless claw
spooning
out the cages of clipped winged birds
where they sing
songs
which come from nowhere
as they imagine
thievery has taken its time
to show up
on a morning day
speaking everything
speaking trust
excused and disguised
do not
leave here
alone
thievery
she assumes the responsibility
that it is not
exactly
the same
again
and thievery has interrupted us
in the Nightingales of cowardly war
that the door should ring
once or not.

Day without you; now, seems so empty
even in this place where I so enjoy to be,
going back to roots to know the clearest way to act
the landscape is so new and it might call us back
to meet again, a hopeful harvest
and the living could be easy
the room is locked and we are, until surrender
invisibility is the power of peace,
may this my dear
stay between you and I,
that the thought of all
has smiled in your eyes.

All I have to do is to arrange a flower bouquet
to look, always, the same way
so that at each awakening
the maps on notes
purposely goodbye
I have not yet met she who
in bliss and perfume
will open sleepy eyes
to the portrait of drying petals
of peeling paint
a fresh mess to organize
never forget
that there once has been a negro speaker
that no one has listened
holding out hands and holding out gifts!
They might be mistaken for marriages
guided by magnetism,
crowds, friends and surroundings
far enough
have eclipsed an angel's apparel
printed daily
into large headlines
folded, afraid, into origami
and under the two glass slates of the microscope
label the lamella "specimen B"
as my hands will be empty
and will still have to do.

I had in mind no secrets
when the waters came down, and broke
we talked and talked all day long
while the rains flooded our streets.
It wasn't planned nor was it supposed
that in such short time
gut(ters) were to overflow into my mind
with their thunderstruck feeling
in which I had never planed to keep any
and any at all,
secrets.

Crippled and out of place
and laces untied
tripped, is a gamble
but I have no time to tie
I have many knots already,
keeping my barge from drifting off.

now try me better than before
ready to get even with *unwealthy* score
what is so easy to do
my head has noted and agreed to
but now, and further on
I have in mind nothing that would hide
any time or region uncharted
with your hands on my skin, glide
in my thoughts no secret is wanted.

As I wash the *sulfury* smell off my skin
I am a firework which soon will burn
up
into the barely temporary amusement
which you have known
for the last few days
the plane has travelled so far as to let me off
without a warning,
a wading promise,
floating near the edge
let the rescue
cry out in pain
to fly off
how long would last this or any
let us wed
in the birth of a nation
cary out that
it will not be long before she reappears
dazzling showers
a distracted body
grasping onto liberty

You know the machine will roll and come and fabricate
that everything it has known, it ate
the devoured franchise deep fried in
common and walk along,
the wheel keeps us going
forward or wrong
anyplace is better than prehistory
because maybe they will in fact remember
the one who was richer than everyone else
the machine will keep on going
winning.
Never will we wait
to catch a fish
come back to the side of clumsy protests
what it must be a good bait
to distract them
from the light that shines
I'm *gonna* let it
tell apart the cogs
shining well greased
by every employee's bills
and will keep on rolling,
red of the steam rooms and flags
stop to fill the tank

Roam to tell apart the culture
which you have been lacking
the song with which you still have not
the basses and bottoms
feed the lending patrons
crowning figures with haloed crowns
and wallpaintings, picturesque
are you ready to be a soldier?
Marching agains the tides of concrete
as they try to eat your body
in morsels of crumbs
do we bottom feeders strive
to contaminate them with the plague
horses inviting fleet
roam to read the scriptures and earn degrees
to hooves will turn your feet
offspring the crews of stealth
manning cares of the next empire

to hooves will turn your feet
tablets well in hand
collect the siblings of what you are
if it is easy to tell
yourself from your fellow men
if you can say you are
distinct.

I wrote something a few weeks ago.
Sometimes I read it over and I like it,
Sometimes I read it over and I think it's shit.
I guess it's kind of like my life.
A little more effort might be necessary
a little more give and take
try tasting words
to know how foul your fucking mouth is
try eating MacDonald's.
Is there anything around here that is not truly disappointing if you think
about it
is there a person who is not truly ugly if you look at how people are
if you ever want to kill your boner, try to overthink it, and look at her
forehead
how fucking random is a forehead
how disgusting and useless is hair; a remnant of our idiot ancestors
how ugly are bald people, like a newborn foetus
crying its ugly red face to tears
think of how disappointing our species is,
we are doing worst than our idiot ancestors.
I guess it's kind of like my life.
Sometimes I take a walk and appreciate the nice landscapes, and the
weather.
Other times I get fucking bored.
What distinguishes one sun from the other
how much you slept, how much you dreamt
how much you want,
and to shake your lazy bones,
I guess it doesn't matter anyway
to lay there and get the same as everyone else
crying like the still newborn foetus

crying at some light
to know what despise feels like
try to overthink it,
and I thought of this some years ago,
sometimes I go for a walk,
I guess it's kind of like my life.

Fruits of their tropical progress
here come the ships with merchandise to consume
use them up
there is more where that came from
to a trap the coin way
we might use you to make them
and tam-tams are the metronomes
which count the beats
the whips are cracking the picking hands
beware from behind your will is a samba
back and forth from two parties
one leading and, surrenders
she to the authority of the leaders
until the working woman
will climb her way back up
from the baskets upon her back
there is a lot more where that came from
have some broth and go to bed
we will give you songs in the morning
they will be in the same tonalities
as the bells ringing, chains clink
take up the cook-pot and, all of it, drink
all of it will boil over
so that there will be no more viruses,
no more germs,
so it will be potable

hymns of the red brother
banging on his skin drum the feathered hair
or styles have banished from publicity,
has hammered on the flags
has waved it over victorious heads
and whom the propaganda has ripped to shreds
the reputation that the world now dreads
sing with Lenin's men
who have removed the folktales' threat
as they always knock thrice
when kingdom come
flying with nuclear regrets
have they slandered
and the tension
has gone on too long
spread the word if you will
cooperate with thought, discussion
and me,
friend,
and the definition of comrade
and coworker

Thinking I want to get fucked up
experimenting with hard drugs
maybe try some cocaine
maybe it'll make me kill someone
maybe I'll do what I wanted to do all along.

Not even wanting to be around myself is a problem
to live with
for those who don't want to murder their hopes and dreams
call upon illegal substances.

To think that taking everything was legal before last century.
To think that before no one gave a damn.
To think that today, a lot of people still don't.
Deep inside, what do we all care.

Maybe I'm afraid that they will make me appear clearly
to act out my every thought
most people do not want to get in so deep
as to forget what they did
what they would not remember
if their lives were still so dull
under their own
righteous
grid.

Once more on the verge of suicide
drinking hot chocolate and eating fried chicken
what is there going in life
besides regrettable *unachievements*
and thoughts that cannot be communicated
you handicapped idiot
you've burned all of it
in the time and space you hate
in the time and places you hate
you still fear and dread going back
even for a beer with friends.
Keep on moving to places new
you will not worry about killing yourself
once you've seen the whole world through.

I *wanna* make a living selling my sex
drunken and indifferent, it's all the same
they can ride my ass
they can shove their dirty genitals in my face
give me the turf on which
artificially we get milk
chemically we grow corn
chemically we make sugar
artificially we get satisfied

I want to be a prostitute to whom people come in the darkness of
headlights
who calls out to dirty roaming coats
who shows some leg, shows some pecs,
I want people to come to me
for their every fantasies

buy my body and I will not be repulsed
not be uninterested
I will not quit, will not weep
give me a condom, I will kiss your every inch
I will suck on your repressed needs
on your repressing media
as I do on your local mayor, on your priest,
on your mothers
let me sell me to you as I've sold myself to others
buy me
I want to make on living
to keep my living
I want to make you feel
and own it.

I who am forgotten by your clocks
who is behind
who is jealous
wants to be
anything else
then here, and your little bitch
wants to be something proud, something of a bird,
wants the best of the world
in the muck,
in the diseases
the insanity, the apocalypse, collapse
twilight dusk
and the gloomy eyes,
soaked with bodily fluids on the bathroom floor
where are my pants, my panties,
forgotten by a place to return to sleep,
enough time underground, enough and now the hunter
the hunter has the hay and the matches
and is hunting out the badger
and badgers bite.
Forgotten by time passing and sheets of beds broken
you have made it harder than it had to be
you thought you were ugly, I was into you
Now I have some rum you should enjoy
look into the needles of pupils that spin around
kiss my bleeding lips
bitten through the skin
taste the sour and bitter leech
look into the regrets that spin around
and burn it all to the ground.
In an orgy,

where the salvation army unleashes its cross
charity has the limits of willingness
and you too can be scorned
forgotten by clocks
besieged by patrols in the night paranoia
choose instead to spit in their faces
speak with those worthless drunks
and become one of them
without shyness
tired of being your drug-free self
you would get used to being a wise man
if you would have been passed and over
much more than you can eat
has been cooked and served in silver dishes
and it all looks so good
for how long will you stay seated
getting fat
gluttonous amnesia of LSD
tripping for the end of the day that does not matter
wreck your life
take my rags
I will bathe in the cold glacial river
forgotten by your clocks

<u>fog of the morning you</u>

First toe in, the water ripples
do not believe that time is crippling
if glacial earth must thaw
then collapse the lips around your nipples
to new weather we are adapting
truthful words sent, you just saw

swam the swans of gliding feathers
white as flocks due north fore snow
eiderdowns for pairs of luggage
poems from romances of our elders
rejoining now, where railway docks row
lips have locked no need to forage

if glacial earth must never be again
to the fires may we together dance, then
if memory must try to enhance
to pursue the certainty of a perfect stance
let it lead to blissful madness
of which slavery will be seen as a stepping stone
where cracks will form in every bone
with etched in hope one senescent address

plunged in a bath of a still lake
away from the wind's chilling voice
let it convince the many birds
but shivers shall we not flake
and mermaid of my choice
drown me as all I've heard.

wake up with nausea and work through it
anything can be done afterward's will
and then rest rid all ill
even cure feverish sighs
through your shirts and sheets have soaked
wake up feeling the day before
the bad beer and the bottom of the well
falling from where you were face first flat on the floor
wake up with bad dreams, with itches, gnawing
growls and hunger from your mouth and
raise your voice ever so louder
there is inside a cynical humour
to laugh the laugh of maniacal boundaries
because better shall be the forward of strong souls
they will crush, and spit, and bother you
wake up with nausea at the sight out the window
    to the work that dries your hands' skin
    the worries that make no day end or begin
stronger than guards
and work through
a smuggler's happiness

It had been quite a while
until I once more had no idea where I was going
until there were a thousand paths in the ocean waves
and my C.V. applied to every job,
where would come the call
it had been quite some time
before I felt everyone was an unstable friend
and my skin could be a blanket
and I could find myself a whore
to fall in love with until I went.

Where they do not ask my papers
in the dungeons and sky scraping attics
pretending that the life is made
with the sweat of my brow

and it had been quite a while
so help me go back to wandering
to go back on a catapult of a thumb
the miles I've ridden for free
without a ticket
with no identity
it had been a long time
until I had wished I lost interest,
that I was not attached to anything in my magnetic environment
but grasping my drowning breath
I had comfort(.)
until weakness withed footsteps
the line is yellow and the call for the next
a passport is everything as long as they take it
the stamp is only pressed if handed it was

until tropics you have missed and ice you have seen
until you still ride away from home
and you never find one best
rhythm in the speak and the socializing box
with a harmonica on one of the four corners of a four way intersection
well frankly it's not something you've waited for
to once again be cold and on the floor
blow your nose and get up when the alarm does not ring
but your C.V. is for every job
with the Spanish and the Polish knocking on the doors
if they all want the first world so go in reverse
and have the crapy job in Jakarta
it has been quite a while
since you've thought about how things are
and there are no signs
but thank you for *havin'* taken interest
in the last hours of the day you have heavy eyes
and new ideas with snapping dragon bites
fishing the streams of a wild America for trout
dying in Alaska for the gaze of envious contemplative "middle-class"
wondering where she went
until prehistory is a discovered table to decipher
a spring torrent suddenly floating the house from flooded base-
ment up to its sails
and as a pirate with a skull on a black flag
plunder the possibilities that others would take if they could
in a system of nobility and born riches
who is to tell what is whose
and it's been quite a long time
before I stopped caring
until I wanted to stop caring
it's been quite a while,
until I started doubting once more
until I had no idea of any worth.

There was a new word on the cutting board
the orphans were asking for food or parents with whom they
could starve
the junkyards were asking for junkies
the trash piles were asking for recycling
the needles were asking for doctors
and with a very sharp cooking knife
with the stir fry round is popping oil
stories will be told
fondly of course, palming proudly what we have done
and from where we come
in other words: what we have no choice to be proud about
and its letters were all so succulent
some parts were sweet and others not quite
and how it was served was a real delight
it gave all the character
cooking a new word is such matter!

It's like a forest that has dried out and suddenly appears ablaze
and I will sleep in a bed of charcoal
the homeless animals crying at large
lost in the shipwrecked barge at sea
as they wave their colourful cloths
to dust rising smoke
black in the atmosphere
not knowing
that those are
their siblings .

Suddenly the raven's claw
seems to be the one in aw
can cursed be the winds have blown
and the ax held which you now hone
feared and dreaded for nights without news
Irony sure can amuse
the feathers black are on their way
widows need now not pray
as cut open is the truth
there are no saints to whom commute

"please do not leave me, please do not go"
there is so much more than I can show
with brilliance and fire and being so sweet
hear the laments, the drums I beat
plead now for war so off can go the people whose deaths would
pardon all your sorry
with *them* will keep on going so much more than (both) your story?
Kiss them now the goodbye smooch
need not please the now no more
"please do not leave me" is but a mooch
others can find at the corner store
and with a dime in your right hand
between your thumb and forefinger
choose the new candy which would make you feel grand
kiss him well, to forget what may linger
let tears be the problem of the one who cries them.

If she rose now I would be disappointed
that the sea has just calmed
and that my conscience is now guilt free
dripping of sweat, soaking my clothes clench to my body,
dripping with sweets
beaten as a piñata around the bush when
last night finally a word has been said
or wasted
off of cocktail mixed-drinks
everyone saw the moment
when ignition took off, took with it
and in waiting,
this had been so nice,
and soundly have slept,
soundly have looked upon a still dreaming face
gigantic moments will boast the telling of the tale of
the life time only goes on
from one node to another
as a sentence may be understood
small thing to small moment, one is to another
as breathing or remembering her laughter
with red lipstick and the look in her eye
from one point to another
fuelling and driving under influence
takes a turn to another drunk text,
to let her know
when she rises
and I would be disappointed
not to have an exit to
live out this attempt
at formulating

a number to reach
a next date
chance encounters
don't go.

That fuck lacking bitch
she has blocked the road that stretched across
the gorge,
and on one side childhood at its nursery's peak
and on the other,
a city shimmering with neon signs
for there is no bedtime,
and sexual ecstasy is just
one self destructive liberation away
where breath is something of sudden whisper
opportunity's dropped clues for the needy and the need
for where there is a starving guru
he would not decline afternoon tea.
And she would not lend a hand,
nor a hand nor a lip
and though she herself watches rolling hips wandering off past the
hills
and they will not come back as hard as she wills them to
she will watch photographs of men in their suits of leather
that fuck lacking bitch she will,
bark at the kids with flowers in their hair
with boots ornamented with heavy metal studs
she will call them names because of their bracelets and
them being new to the system
they would not know more
than their instinct
to kiss each other,
and nibble their necks.
And what they've been taught
to make the lights shimmer, to make them go on and off
to sit on the other side at a pole or a counter

soon enough they will be walking by again
asking about names to give
to perhaps a heathen.

And once again I lay awake
and soon the morning sky will quake
out of a rising sun
with its orange peeled vapours
torn white where night will end.

Rock me in my sleep
cradle of the morn's events
and a wake is the forward state
on which our infrastructure's built
its coin, its tracks, its way of life
which open eyes look to in the dark
and tuck me in mother land,
with a sheet and a blanket
to be warm inside your reserved privileges
tuck me in, take me by the hand,
tell me a nice story where there are no monsters to harm
to want to take it all,
to pocket souls as a good luck charm
rock me in the cradle where we all wish to keep lying
and to keep in sniffling into tissues white cocaine
me asleep, a wake in dreams I had
and an open coffin
the guy I never knew
rock me in my sleep, whipping hair
back and forth with a loosened head
the parties have the power
they should never go out
ruining yourself independently
with no support for your amendments
and it's never too careful,
to take a bunch of drugs
all alone.
And you can add more music,
something to chant a hymn with,
the girls can dance and drag you to the floor
and you can compliment the way they're dressed
awake, forgetting that other bloke

who would enjoy your shoes, to step up and speak
singing along to the music,
as a lullaby to rock, in your sleep
a wake of what was the day
and that is over, again is over,
that you would try to find whenever there is no
mare to bear children realities, and prospected mistakes
or ripped off a single percentage
because it says so in her size, to soon rock to sleep
in the cradle of what would then
the schools, the healthcare, the midwife
and the midlife crisis
there are popes, high on LSD, who tried to bring it all together
but over who, over he, over you, over me
not enough did join the party
rock me in my sleep
vile, disrespected teddybear of mine
who wishes to open state, at the age of thirty,
that they still have the same hopes
coming straight from
at one point in life
when once it meant something more to us,
than most things do to regular people,
been trying to meet you
in a satanic butchered
tongue, and part of a street
with gravities changing meaning
as gangs go out of business
as we wear different chains
and there too, no one knows it's singular
it's a graffito, or it's a panino
no one knows how to go alone, to
the movies, a concert.

There is a bar on the corner
and that is where, weak and scared
and sucking thumb
soon sucking else
the insecure and child-like
the one who would cry for a mommy
who was by side, by side
they go to find a replacement
because they've know their old lady
for much too long, much too long
you've got your good thing
rock me, in an old man's rocking chair
staring at the open suburbs
I will find mine
and rock me, rock me in the nursery
the one we call "basic training"
let me do the job
that needs to be done
let me drive the eight ball with a shaft
a rolled up paper,
feeling the melting powder
as it drips into my throat
out they may flow
let me tell you my name and who I am,
and you are you, you sure look nice
please accept I buy you a drink
and soon you can rock me to sleep
with hair a mess,
and the smell of weed and cigarets,
and ties in the flag's colours
and the knot in the rope
preventing it from rising up
to the top of the pole

and so it appears the dust covered dusk city
the smog scuttling winds,
carrying away what rises some more
in the beacons of routine
to produce as much in a year
we must go to it day by day
and she looks at us in this same way
through her curtains she looks at us,
the tops of minarets and cross-section red lights
green means go,
orange means slow,
night means to sleep
she knows not our worries
she is the morning greeting and a trophy wife
she has her say in this world
she is the mother of our children
she is our mom on the top of her small throne
and today will be same as before
with no research reading or beast
the wind will carry what keeps on coming
and soon enough we will be painting suns
to remember what is not there no more
and we will soon enough be painting sons
because she needs to take care
and she cannot join us at work because she is
not to know those worries
because she is to be a trophy
orange means slow and she cooks our breakfast
in the streets there are
jive cats talking their minds and it could
offend the old bourgeoise in her house
offend her at the top of her respectable ignorance
was she brought up for more

than to be slept with
smog clusters of clouds and cover the blasting rays of
watches in the tight traffic,
each booming towards a respectable, productive, force,
to be a part of
a standardized view of society
yet some women went out to earn their wages
to be wept on, to be swept with
to be secretaries, to be slept with
blown smoke about by (imported) "Havana" cigar establishment
men in the street, honking their
whistling lunch breaks in the beaten hats
car horns,
honking streets
and good living
breathing in
the garbage thrown back
because it could be thrown out.
And she is looking behind her curtains
afraid of new, afraid of youth
afraid to dance, and of crime, and of change
and of changing away with the time,
wrinkling her night shirt stuff into a suitcase
going on a trip to Florida
where you do not need a passport to bask in the same
which is obscured by the everyday
in which she is
waiting
slowly
to go.

A harmonica playing hobo
was siting next to the train station,
dabbling on songs he had made up himself
because he had to say it somewhere
without being ashamed of how people understood
the complaining thought of a hard life
it's hard on all of us,
but confusion takes its toll
on the ones who have it worst.

Don't call us cursed fleabags for dragging our sorry selves across
the country
on nothing more than a thumb
hope for good will at the soup kitchen
where a new life in the slopes of hard work, and hard pay
and the temptation to have fun only to have a bed
and not in the snow to lay, face down
with the love of a hooker, in the same universe,
perhaps she did feel pity
rowing across the Styx with only eyelids to pay with
and now cry to keep from burning, cry as they row
eat up your bread and drink up your soup
as you live on skid row.

Repent you filthy scumbag!
Admit that you have cheated,
that you have lied and held knives
and that in the back of your dearest peers
a drawn tongue has sought to mutilate
the depressive representative of another race
where once mermaids had lived
holding up opportunities and commerce
but with the once noble goal of helping
blinded by self assurance,
being something of an experimented
and you historians
reading books and guessing theories
in the first stage,
dancing the same sharpened tools
and you will be surprised
when you will notice your name
on the list into satan's circle
just and high, getting by
say what is and had been wronged
shame sharpened sculptures
depicting moments of heroic
betrayal in depths of pictures
staining constitutions for generations
to remember how neglected we've made ourselves
and we *maid* ourselves to clean
by teaching to not become
the pictures of murderous scum
to the environment deprived of surface
of the surface to block out
repent.

"scum society" is the term we should use for our capitalist society
for the slight percentage of algae, the scum which floats on top,
cuts of the sun, and lets the environment underneath slowly die.
the scum society is the one
where what lies on top, kills off what's lower
occupying the gold-sunlight rich surface

I did not say that, no, it was not my will
do not interpret what I say, do not
I will do it for myself
but I did not make this reservation
yes it is my name
now you will think what I cannot stop
though remember it was not my doing

do not act upon my be-half for my whole will do
and if I must correct your actions
than I will be halved too
and your wish be done

thank you for trying to be useful,
thanks for attempting niceness
though it was not my wish, it was not my want
I did not say exactly that
do not imagine my words.
Language is precise for that specific reason
not open to interpretation
not it was not my will
do not blame me for it
do not blame me
for what others have done in my name.

Crippling cold I feel inside of me
where do you come from and why are you here
is there a way to chase
to reach a moot point of
disinterest and indifference
where I am neither in love
nor do I care
nor do I want to help or cry or rage
but to be a little independent particle
to be tossed in the wind, a spec,
kindling to ash under the ambers of the fire
what did charm me I do not know
Why think about you,
you are a tiresome worry
of a cripple
starring out the crystal clear window
and questioning a crystal ball
in a dark tent of fortunes and wonders
forgiveness in the cards,
an image in the crystal ball
and euphoria of the carnival
with the lights in the dark and prizes to be *one*
to climb to the top of the city the horizon to see
in the wheel of fate
and the wheel of fortune
which we had invented to make it easy
to flip a coin the decisions are harder
so when they land our choice is made
the night has gone clean
and I'm cold as I open my eyes
the carnival has left town.

spare the feelings of any newborn villain
may he wish the harshest revenge
upon all who might wrong and will
out of a common nature
up, upon a falling star
angel of revolt ,
with free will given not to obey
and condemn to the *shame* as him
he who would disagree such common values
to forage the first berries
be they edible the better.

I will cheat nothing in the wrestling
and rustling bushes
where the simplest things can be the
information delivered as a once in a life
time to move and get away to get to get
away, away is the only time and place where
we know what is and what surrounds us now
so we can think
to what will the little people we once were
will want to wish to then prefer
as a toy, a song, a book with pictures to hoard
in the den of fire breathing "we"
to whom will the message be
the lines of the tombstone epitaph
with large rims and a hat to block out the sun
the deserted skull in the middle of nowhere
we could be on some painting of the zones,
known for being arid, and warm
and nothing or no man nothing
because altitude, because distance and scarcity
is the first thing to be noticed
and to be prayed for
or built a machine for mana or of Kalevala quests
songs lost and put back together again
no man could ever deny wanting to eliminate worry
for fearfulness now elects different views every year or so
and that even once the technical dreams
are now trembling in the fortified backyards
nothing more to be done but to kiss
on every inch
the outstretched skin of bodies and snakes

when the dust will be to bite
just as we've bitten earlobes and *hineys*
and the honeysuckles shall grow again
where the bushes rustle fresh and
we fearlessly stretch out our hands.

Thistle has grown here and there
and soon enough will we see it bloom
the fields we've crossed now everywhere
and how good is the feeling of coming back to thee
home of the once only god
the only map the line at the end of the pointing index
as we can laugh at other customs
we can speculate on different space
and the spring as well is of this celebration
there has been an alignment of welcomes
the first to raise its head to call out to the mournful
to awaken the children of the dead
who, themselves, will not live past one year.
Thistle is a flower all have encountered
when it turns purple or blue
when you are, in a place, new
when colour charms your eye
and the townsfolk have not been careful
their watch not too bright
their customs are so precious
they've begged with closed hands
to me who was born in a house that stands
still at the end of the street
where plants also have flourish again and to
the lady who does not fear sharp corners
sanding is the art of nature
who can adapt, can survive, can hunt
can as some walk to the next map's owners
can as, how's been their pasture
and be not so blunt, no, be elegant
they like flattery, they like bright colours

when bloom the thistles' rounded flowers
hand the lady a tale
that has drawn before

There's been
on the sunniest days
going back and forth
the fields and home
on the hottest days
where shade is a best friend
and no one scares from their shadow
a lot of
on the sunniest days
envying the one who has food to eat
and a ticket for the railcar
who does not have to worry
who does not mind the envious
and the jealous
which is why they are
but he works hard
on the sunniest days
and he's earned like all have
earned, and they work hard
all, carrying their tools
over their shoulders
to look, or in the rearview mirror
have built lots
have built the train tracks
have made the locomotives
and have ridden and driven and watched the railcars
on the sunniest days
have been happy to
lose worry
get a peaceful mind
don't feel exploited

don't feel ripped off
there are no bad people
you've got food to eat
and you're out on your feet
on the sunniest days

I've been meaning for some time now to get back where it's
warm
where barren lands greet my exiled body
and where echos drown out in the slithering
where winds brush the dunes into crescent shapes
and out of their birth, to head somewhere else
transparency and glass of their sudden fusion
and poor me the steaming quench
retches turning around
somewhere
there must be a proud acre of land
that has never known a human footprint
so that I can look at it from afar
and leave it be.
I've been planing for some time to walk
without sunscreen
as I would have seen it come up
above the windmills and the last road to have harboured my
sailing self, sails in the heart of determination
barely floating after a storm of rain and waves to engulf
the metres high of the vessel, climbing and climbing
to the other cycle of the crescent shapes
and the moon will turn around
and sometimes she, herself, will not even be there
and will grant us the charity
of not being noticed, and of being in her blind
discretion -

The proud tops, the mountain tops, the wide, open, gazers
and there stood before us some people in blazers
their mouths smoking and steaming, with papers full of words
say you more than that with which you cannot argue
of that line of people there are but too few
contest, contesting and win the prize
with red flags in the wind of a fair
in the colourful evening, music and carnies
people of the road must sooner or later spin the loop
of the first lain earth,
fallen tops into their spiteful selves to spit out
and cover
and recover the arable ground with a clean slate, a fresh start
a flesh scar, a wound, to try and flood all the way to the never
melting glaciers,
slowly feeding the streams of culture!
Never again and never
under estimate with the caricature of rapid portraits
with tickets for a bear, sleep with the teddy too
his image in your room, she who never lets portraits of anybody
onto the dresser set the clock for early morning raise the proud top
(of the), and contracts specify the check-in time
and signed the bottom to the every – morning – dress shirts
smoking to release the mid-day breaks.

Constantly investing
their words and their meaning
by the hour, by the minute
they are counted and strut us by in their fancy cars
with golden hub caps,
with noisy mufflers
mum's the word which can break
the cross-eyed beginning
of what is ever more in use

I love you,
and here is a bank of the North's wealth
which grows and can only be touched to perhaps
make it larger, and longer, and speak of dreams
of Tolkien's realm which had reached
our common grounds.
I will say again, I love you
constantly investing,
our common grounds,
to say again,
in the tongue of the only infinite source
In the Bhagavad Gita's length
there is more than existential thought
but let's learn what we need.

And you, there is in regularity
the capable hands of carpenters
who build the stairs, the idols, the alters
who answer prayers in halls of Loretto,
Santa Fe, New Mexico
who drive under the warm sun,

to breath at night
the particular situation
the time made decisions
of the portrait of a princess
dragging her long skirt
along steps.
I love you
without a map,
without a star to guide
wandering under the thunder's roar
without a sun to be a dial
and going forward to find out
adventures.

This distance is a terrible thing
I feel for you
the same bond that lingers through the roots that link us to
the basics of the mountain dew,
the flows of dreams and science through
we need it to live to understand
that we exist

sanctified beyond
dear logic, of which I'm so fond

the siren floats amusing hymns
not sure where it all began
she bought herself a useless man
in timely ways there are no borders
the traps are set so long before
let's not lose any time more
the portrait drawn I made the bed
I love you,

Dear, I love your smile
which distracts me when looking
the fires rise the tea is boiling
and removes all else that which we crave .
I love your cheeks
on which I've lain more than meagre
the reached out oath on books lie finger,
my hand on your ribs which I adore
I've so wanted to hold before
yet you have known that -
and the window is open

it's seen as much
it can be sent unceasing
and on my back carry
what may once more bring direction
there is an idea in my mind
I love you, Dear
when they shovel off the dirt
the nameless wreck will hold
left behind, the goodbye sold
with staggering latency

Man, I'll tell you about this friend,
he's a badass motherfucker, he is
I have to say I admire him for speeding boldly
and not slapping a goddamn care while eating his breakfast
and using terms like "swag" in hip ways while keeping a laid-back attitude
not judging the feeble too severely too openly
knowing it's a quick fall to being a sad motherfucker,
he's just being good in general,
with popular words being a constitution for the social network
a good book in the face of the general public
joining forces with those whose forces can be joined
and mellowing them out around a joint
which does not stop him having an opinion!
No, let me tell you,
he's more informed than any of those "burning bridges" types
so strong, barricading themselves in some separate club,
pointing fingers of spreading their wise speeches
forgetting that somewhere, other folks are hanging out!
He never forgot that lesson we learn after the first few fights
to roll with the punches
and to float in the waves, not to drown in them!
If punches be tossed, I even think he would win!
But if he were to loose man, I'll tell you,
even those with different ways
they would step up to ask what the hell was going on
and pick him up to his own two feet,
and cuss upon that sucker who got furious and aggressive!
Fuck that other guy, man!
I'd rather talk over popcorn and a little dope
than over a switchblade!

It's our goddamned anniversary dear!
I was going to indulge with you the cheapest delicious chocolates
from a store, without any fancy to it
as for so long we have not been picky
and we would have gone on for a long time
enjoying these small things, these small every day things
but instead I am keeping it for tomorrow
this ordinary
for, instead, I will drive with you
and sing at the top of my lungs, while you join in, I hope,
our song,
and dive into a canyon
where the sky will be clear
and the free fall will be dramatic
to measure every free fall upon
a shelf as a cast treasure
hunted for
through the years
it's our anniversary, and notice I did not forget
In the morning we will feel nothing
and creeping from the backseat
in the glove compartment
that breakfast I kept instead
giveth thy daily bread
as we lay
thrust into
this constance
of precipice.

How I miss going hiking, I miss
having a heavy pack on my straight back!
Something I never would be able to cary in my arms
as macho as they are, forested with dark old growth outdoorsy
male hair
with a sleeping bag, a tent, matches, a buck knife and even a gun!
I don't normally put up the tent, I prefer looking up
when it's all clear, but that's the issue!
So often it would rain, but then you put up the tent, keep the pack
pretty dry
and then there would be no fire to cook the food by
that's ok, rare meat, raw meat, it's all the same.
Up north I recon' you could kill the animal and eat it right away
no worries,
and I miss feeling earth under my stable foot, in my worn out shoe
and it would slither, and a balance would be needed
find a balance, you would need
to miss the outdoors
to go back
as to everything you've missed and which has disappeared!
Into an apartment block or the parking lot of a supermarket, shopping mall
you double click the remote-controlled car keys and hear it beep
stuff them back into your stretch-pants stained by Cheetos which stain
because it's not easy when you keep both eyes on the TV as they say
the flabby material sticking to the flabby sweaty ass that once wore jeans!
Boot cuts or regular cuts; who cares as long as it can go through a
thorn bush
without getting ripped to shreds, ripped in a gym – that used to be
the hill.
Go up the hill with your car to sweat wearing different stretch pants,
the view is basically the same!

Darn tutin' life is swell
when you've got your wheels and your credit card I tell you
though there is always a moment when you go to place your six-packs
in the garage
and the old machete calls you
and for that moment, you, the I, the third eye in the third person, we
miss the outdoors and it gets to the ego, the I, the we, with a machete,
like the Spanish *ma-chay-tay*
feeling less of a man, those I watch
except I have TP to wipe with
and a smoothly waxed chest
which I suppose women love! Of course they do, people say they do.
And then I get over it, and can eat my mac' n' cheese

Remembering when you were just a young lass
condemning sex and men, and any politics at all
not knowing what to wish for and not looking for an answer
waiting for it to come out of a church or a wedding ring
dropping out of the sky, a bombing angel with dreary eyes
checking your name on some sacred list
and unpleased by your physique you would be on your guard
hoping the angel would not be a pervert with a trick up his sleeve.
What is a pervert? Why according to you every freak lurking
around
with a match in a canon powder will
and an experimental attitude
giving the absolute truths they all – as you have – ignore and repel
with words and sticks and finally bombing angels
blue for shows and a black fascist shirts for service
camouflage as assailants promise their behaviours
with a flag for a secret list
and they will cross off those who have gotten to heaven
with a powerful sacred orgasm to rip their throats
tip-towing daggers and bayonets in night clubs
come on honey, come on and dance with me
nothing's gonna happen with proper buyer's concern and remorse
it's programmed for obsolescence just like your opportunities
and when your age will be broken you will try to reclaim it
at some consumer service holding onto a fountain's youthful
guarantee

and thank goodness you've changed!
Now when we meet I no longer need to fake a smile
casing in the forged cheques of your back-handed commented
full-out insults

and now we can have a normal conversation!
And when you ask me how I have been,
while you are now going through deep realizations
took me by the hand and boots and both eyes many years ago
they did
I've had a wonderful time!
Childhood being childhood
coexisting with the bearded folk
folklore's grim grasp
it'll catch us up
o'er a thin line!
And people they're used to dreaming
you wake up and go to work
nonetheless soon enough your weary head
it'll wanna play some more.

Always comparing ourselves to others
and to others reacting,
reaching to touch the godly auras
or inevitable betrayal, disappointment,
and *unmendable* wounds
being the deceived by whom, else
than another lie to not fall into despair
claiming to be the best
repeating that we aren't bad
to stand up
and face the days
I do not know what pain this is
but I want it to last,
as long as it can.

Always saying we are more or less
than ever before
laying passed out on the floor
wearing our best friend's partner's perfume
on our body
on our breath
dragon's hoarding away
behind *unpenetrable* scales
played by harps of revered forgiveness
why are they so much?
it's because kidding ourselves is easier
when we aren't the only ones
always to another
comparing the same people
with the same barter

Destinies are linked by kisses like ours,
when their meaning exceeds time
and sudden realization that have disappeared hours
to think that happily I am all thine
and that our ways do better rhyme
so it will all work out fine
so it will all be you and me
I will listen to you everyday
my love, let's be together as it unravels
and everything makes sens
to lock our hands, our mails, our vows, our chains
fastenings of hasty makeshift
not to loose the now opened window's gains
opportunist as is every moment,
and every thought-out decision
in gambling there is precision
and calculations
and to migrate from subject of a nation
to its deliberate participant
and to walk outside without fear of judging eyes
and if to lay in the grass is the intension
then let us discourse with the serpent
for what has been given
glows in the mutation of matter
and care.

The reason why I don't go to bed early is that
if I do then I wake up in the middle of the night, and end up
sleeping less time
          than ever would I have if I were to have crashed at the last
possible moment
to be living the next day.
Just let it go and kick it along the street
a tossed out can will still end up
being played with is so good so keep on playing
find what you like and keep on until the wee hours
until your eyes burn red and the sun is rising
and the only choice of time is nothing but ours
find your energy, just find it and keep on going
and crash when you're empty, crash when you're out
when there is no more reason to be up and about
when there is some fire running low
and the smoke is dirtying your house
you touch the walls and your hand turns black
don't force yourself you'll just burn out
the reason why I never try to turn in before
crashing is the nature of science
there is no gravity, will there be a force
inside me it's all floating loose
there's all a fuss about what goes where
there is a date printed on my forehead for when I expire
sadly I can't see it
just keep dining and take your time
it's better for you, it's better for your health
you don't want to end up with a busted butt and being stabbed
you don't want to lose any sense of priority
never taking no bull but never trying to sell some either

wanting to make a fortune from anything at all
the red dawn's over, it's the era of the fall
it'll all grow back now trust me
the seasons they go around
take a plane boy, take a trip, in other places they think differently
and it's sure that their climate will get to us
disturb the gulf stream and there is one tough winter coming
it's a strong current, it'll drag you out to sea
surely others will leave also to try to find a meaning
and keep on going until of home you dream
you have to trust, you have to trust
that when you really have to crash,
you will sleep the most comfortable night
and wake up full of life
have fun, man.

Later is always later
for later constantly postponed
when will then stop?
Later is always later
no use for the tools you've honed
that from the shop the best had bought
later is always later
to dream of the people that others have boned
ain't silent hope that'll get 'em to stop
later is always later
and live by what others have loaned
not knowing if you can handle a mop
later is always later
saying that more is had than what is owned
wanting it real but the lie can't drop
later is always later
wanting it bad but it can't be clowned
no results out of nowhere's pop
later is always later
and too late is soon fully blown
and still be eating the same slop
later is always later.

she scares me as does what matters
when the earth itself as anything shatters
I will still mumble that I love her.

I love you either ways if you go or stay,
but if you stay I can cherish you.
I love you at the beginning of the day
when from home each one goes his way
only to come back in the evening or at dusk,
and when we do, I can cherish you.
And when alone lies the soul of one or the other
when it craves the caress of an embracing late spring
forward with arms open I will hope my words remember
that my heart beats for no other
than for a second of hearing your presence
and to come back to it when I languish
to breathe again lightly,
I will cherish you and in hopes and wish
and give my all for you to see
I will cherish you

We, who had been friends for a long time,
stone drunk on the outskirts of that party, had started smooching
and when I thought about your man, a nice man,
I asked what we were doing my mouth on your neck
and you looked at me with grey eyes
; all the pretence does erase regret
all the self convincing does brainwash our guilt
and before we took off our clothes and we were but lies
just friends, and your man somewhere, and me as flawed as a
bachelor is
and others raising their glasses to better see further than their
noses just into their   mouthes
cheers to spill into each others' cap
to be sure that nothing is poisoned
I am sure that you are not poisoned
"I am sure that this is good"
that none will tell and that no rip will be torn
and no one will be reborn
and nothing new will actually come to light
our lips have locked and so we are finally here
after pondering for so long, running past green highway signs
indicated in lengthy miles just to throw us off
you looked at me with gray eyes that wanted victory but feared a
fatal crash
looking for an idea alternative to sink into
to live "that one that got away" just in front of us to reach out and grab
and that our curiosity is deadly or not, is not for us to know
it's for us to try out, sober or intoxicated, disregarding any previ-
ous theory
to disprove as the greatest scientists we try to zero gravity on earth
to make it into the hall of fame of Nobel laureates

and to have the other hang around our necks for as long as
possible,
to feel safe and rich and important
and that we have
for as long as your grey eyes
and our lips lock
and the sweet autumn breeze wears a merry costume
and my hands stay warm to caress your tight hips.
The street was silent then and in the house they were yelping out
joyful toasts
and you stood close to me
and the street lamps were projecting their yellow fame
and I turned to your cheek
and your ear
not with a whisper

Oh the darkest part of a life,
when we are born we cry and it hurts
What a rush!
Can you compare it to any feeling of victory
inside the boxing ring
you tell yourself and toughen up
still blind with ectoplasm
nothing to remember by
and you take it in!

I don't want to live saying things are awkward
I don't want to stand silent and ashamed
and not knowing why my legs want to run
not knowing how to act day in and day framed
and as the pictures are taken and their portrait hangs still
to feel them fallen and to bring flowers about
and I do not want my throat to swell up
I do not want goodbyes to be a fault and
I do not want to feel like so little was said,
but to know that more than enough was
satisfaction and perfection never comes
and to know they were well spent and the pictures read
in their colours and tones and shapes
I don't want to live saying things are awkward
I don't want them to

How many more friends must I lose
if to say the truth is a reason for farewell
should hypocrisy then stand in my shoes?
Or should I hope that to realize no harm done
never an insult should reality propel
and accept a wrong when wrong a reflex has spun
and apologize,
or pretend as if nothing was.
How many more friends must desert my side
have they been hurt when disagree I did?
I do not hit but respond to their defences
in which attack is often the chosen bride
not that law should be an eye for an eye
but if I am hit then to hit harder is my stance,
but when we lay broken on the floor
consolation will or be no more
that only the truth had tried to shine
not to make hers or yours or mine
but to make ours.
Please tell me that now calm you are,
that after the advice, that of moon and star
you've come to be the smiling face
that only wishes to at stable pace
walk in the same places
where we sometimes meet.

I hope, yes hope I do
that the truth will scare, no, none of you
that you will never desert any spoken word
because at first you laughed when that you heard
but that once clear it is, or fact it gleams

follow that word which you now know
is beyond that of skins we wear

but hope have I that not beware
should I that in pride of self wrong
a friend I had has now long gone.
How many friends have left this table
had eaten the food and now live in fable
and as others haunt faces that cross my path?
How many friends should I be to lose
by saying that which they cannot disprove
which none may, and that fact that makes them laugh
but that shall outlive us all.

Silence or goodbye
is it the same, yes the same sigh?

I have two arms
that will carry my brethren
(full of) hope
over wolds of elevated plateaus
and wastelands
dregs of floodwaters and evaporated prayers
and despair to keep going on
two hands to shake with
the greetings of forward comradeship
and betrayal
and failed ventures
wards of lain down
given up
bodies,
sweating into filth stained sheets,
still, on rusty cots,
spare beds.
The will to wait healing
a throat to shout
to signal danger
to ask for help
ever so aggressive, unpleasant from fear
spears piercing flesh
endangered,
noticed vulnerable
eyes to perceive self
to the others of reaction
to the future of being
comrades, the road paved with necessity
compromise for the time being
thumbs up with later trust

unspoken is the better propaganda
halfway is the distance to back up upon
skin tanning as the sun sets yet not
no sleep in the beds of charity,
burning wounds,
no despair to the bearers of ideals.

I worked that out in therapy
they asked me to tell them what was wrong
when I talked to myself they were afraid
they need a subject, I need an object
will you be the outside cause I define to?
There is something in my pocket for you
you don't wanna catch a cold or something
you don't want to be sneezing and feel so *bleh*
there is no reason to mistreat even the unimportant
or so they say, or so they tell you
as good as they can respond.

To the doctor I pay so much
there is no health plan to cover my brain
where does pre-existence begin?
Can I get insurance for my foetus?
Will I get payed if the bastard has some problem
will it pay a nurse?
It's wise to insure what you decide you need
and fuck those tax dollars,
I will never be needing their services ever more
ever more and since Mohamed spoke
Idiots wrote their souls freezing on the melting ice caps
and in the flames of their own fury and decisive crap
it's better to think things through before committing
it's better to rethink them even then
it's good to find a bed before vomiting
it's good to learn about all when you're ten
it takes time to find what it's about
plant the big picture for it to sprout
you really need to give it some thought

the more time you get to use what you bought
you get to be good, to know the shortcut keys
to learn to bike surely you scrape your knees
and if your elbow gets broken
you go see the doctors, get a cast
you get some pills to chill out
you try it all not to worsen
not loose your hair so fast
guards and helmets, t's'what it's about.
Time to all things
gather what it brings
kick it and chill
no need for ice or heavy commandments
I worked that all out in therapy.

We are so retarded we don't even know,
a century starts out as a dark age
dies as light, glorious, furry, fear.

Debauchery is a consolation prize
something to say you're not alone to try
to find, once more, pleasures
a consolation prize, a here and there compliment
to make one's self feel important,
to feel wanted and that should live
out, a long lasting union (waiting)
is so much more to do
to fantasize with "you", the one
will make it all come true
without the search
the drawn out wait,
the cost-full participation fee
no one looses for free
and despair may build it's temple
in which to pray is a daily ritual
but to win that first place stand
the podium's finger band,
and who will, for you try
as much as eye for eye
whilst the losers then may sigh
I for I's all it's worth
and thought appraisers sometimes, girth
over, they will not buy
and although O rejoice under night skies,
know debauchery as a consolation prize

<u>Everything is fair.</u>
The superfunk jive dripping from my ancestors' graves
they have given me the greatest gift of all
a nice necklace I never would have found in the largest supermarket
I learned some German when I went skiing
and the men told it would be useless
what I've been thinking is that deep the mine shafts had nice jewels
I would prefer to knife someone in the back,
but only if he was an unsuspecting rapist type,
men can see them, spots like blood on a collar,
spots like ghosts out of graveyard fog, don't lie to me,
I know everything you did last daytime

I knew a woman, man, she smelled so good,
it's not like I drowned myself if mud,
It's not like a business could have opened a spa somewhere near,
but I do know a DANCE CLUB WHERE COPS they come and
see us
they usually trade their weapons for pairs of shoes,
I drop that steel in the garbage
it's too bad it's the kind found in the uneducated
crows they call the birds in the trees,
If I were to climb up there they would yell,
cram something down my throat, food does not mean anything to me,
I was bearing chains on the internet, people told
"don't lock yourself up", my ankle bracelet is a mac,
my intense bling bling I call acer,
Ladies, ladies find a man who uses linux, yea yea
he takes the time for the details, he takes the time
I'm just somme greasy man out of a hole in the ground,
I might give you some coal, stay warm or get a diamond,

I stabbed some billionaires, walking in a street unsuspecting,
the cops traded their weapons for body parts,
I wear his foot like a lucky charm
they call me a cannibal, I just like to own and I like it as much,
smack me on the head one more time, hit me upside the jaw,
if I were a cougar, if I were a racist Jamaican man you could
subdue me,
you could not subdue victims,
yea christians would be christians
it's probably not good but I'm having fun high off dope,
high off some sort of peyote nonsense,
it's probably not good but I'm finding comfort,
like the missionaries and their desert gold, I say gold is always but
a desert,
some people drank that too, turned out dead

I'm not some sort of super agent looking for some mission not to talk
about,
I just like funk music and brushing off my mofro,
I just like to play some ball in the bedroom in the street, in the strip club
believe it or not but it's on the other side of the street from the legion,
yea veterans like it too, don't be so negative about looking
the woods bring so much as my ax it can cut down faster
the machines they came and cut from my yard,
they took the wood and the topsoil, they took my aquifer they took my oil
you could not think of anything better than to leave me a
skatepark,
the stalagmites being the highest ramps in the world,
slipping might become like the new accidental murder,
I prefer to have a billionaire with a blade like I slid a
thought and exchanged it with the lawman attention making,

you think I'm a Zulu? You think I'm a Zulu?
Nah man, I am a friend and not a distant relative,
I am the life partner and the smile of any good American,
and I am the francophone who the clan hates like the night
and burns like the black man, man, ask the Saskatchewan
fransasquoi,
ask the reserve, ask the sqaw who knows what's up not her
man's attention,
I have a car, we have a car, can't we all have a nice vehicle?
They took the wood, they took the topsoil
they took the aquifer, they took the oil,

I can lick frosting off my lips too, are you too good to like a danish,
nah man, I learned some German, I'd go there too,
you'd never known it but architecture is my secret passion,
so I jive and I dance the funky moon walk with my sneakers,
I've got this superfly medallion an open grave, yea yea
you thought I was superficial, nah man
a memory on my chest is as great a hickey, you'd be thinking
this girl, yea, she asked d'you prefer having that black eye or a
hickey?
I go for both, I'm a proud mother'!

They have given me the greatest gift of all is not my life,
it's not I would not cry on my grave, I'd be too busy being cold
I would be some sort of open mouther kiss of mockery,
you cannot cling to my beard, oh yea, fingers get lost,
it's an insult to all barbers but George Clinton, he dyes it,
he is the bass man master sees around corners and knows what I like,
I want the funk I say I want a movement with feeling
a quest of many tribes just going back to dance freeform style and not

with spears in our ears
there have always been those, yea,
has it just gotten worst?
That's it man I wear that necklace show me all you want I'm happy
my mind is not dead, if I'd learn this year man I can't learn the next
I tell you there is another way of just talking
there are woulds, come now there's also *yee* and *wif*
have you ever read Chaucer? That's some heavy fucker.

Take a moment a breath, take a moment and look some other
place and
breathe and wear nice go-to clothing at the risk of abusing the
word "funky"
say you want to sing, say it in a smooth duet voice
like Barry White and his brassiere orchestra, yea,
for all the *unwhite* bastards, and yea, *unwhite* I put this in musical
culture
I don't give a crap my wife she's Brazilian, yea,
and he's a great signer you hear him you feel you want to, his
voice it's so epic it's like a Gilgamesh,
it will mesh with your desire in some incest-filled swamp,
your deformed genes they will get naturalized,
your passed will resurface, will you realize;
DON'T fuck your sister, man.

And then we have a super-dance party with fresh cut apple pier
that's a Canadian dish by the way, and for the win
we just share, thats the point, we drink bourbon and some South-
ern Comfort
and drink Campari with red vermouth,
two together, yea, we take out nationality.

You can fill my head with illusions and nationalist crap
yea, I don't need to get deep and fancy will say and say repeat; crap
I don't ride a pony on the front lines, they suffered enough
today's tea comes from somewhere's else
we will drink it anywhere not for a *geostrategi*,
the climate and weather, it's ok channel, my perfume smells good
anyways
I will not drive to Grasse, and I wont pick them pretty flowers,
wondering of my fingertips will leave a mark,
the pray will re-constitute it,
they will think the criminal is the same man who stabbed a couple
of billionaires

don't you call me soap squeaky clean,
I don't care about food and I will wash myself like people in the middle
a river and a waterfall, can I just lay there for hours,
I can get bitten by snakes, thats cool,
I will dance away and have nothing about lying down cold
I won't, no no no, I wont cry about that,
mouth gaping open and like a piper my tongue,
it will have bitten enough motherfuckers, clean or dirty,
of in some street, dismantled and all.

Buying booze on a smokey street at night
the alphabets, I cannot read
to discuss such things I mustn't need my lawyer,
from my living room I can see further than any sunrise
exchanging coins, counting pennies' close,
biting into some good chocolate
nothing could ever move slower,
there, rickshaw driver calling my face
-       but I have no hair, I have no size, I have no gender
I have no description, I will not answer,
I am a ghost in a paper bag,
and to host such Monday fool's mask
they would never guess how I am fast, and precise,
and here, I give to you another ritual,
if I am not discovered
buying booze on a smoky street at night
they call it a wine centre here
no commission to investigate your breath,
here we go by foot
no commission to investigate you name
no inquisition to investigate your morale
I would like three bottles of Imperial Blue Whisky
and for cheap that is,
to be ignored as I would like to
and sit in a bar
in the booth at the end of the room where the ones,
the unnoticeable bastards in their dark moods
their lively inspirations
when a hat is used to hide your eyes,
and to steady your hands
and to focus your eyes on your hands

and your collar is popped up so your neck is out of sight for any sociopath
and vampiric perversion hiding
and to be ignored in a dark a gloomy tavern
where for all you care it could be crawling with rats and spiders,
and you could have stayed at home if only
and if only, you could stand the silence.
Each ache is a summit I have climbed,
buying booze on a smokey street at night;
this is an open prayer for every moron to go out before the white house,
this is a prayer to teach those morons
Americans are stubborn they say,
because they think that they know what they mean
-       but they don't mean jack shit
when a woman has *accused* Obama of being a communist,
(an accusation or a compliment)
I will accuse her of being an idiot.
And buying booze on a smokey street at night
passing by my gender,
passing by opportunist movies
hitting strange disorders
-     I ran away from North America,
because elsewhere ass-holes are educated
and because when I debate a point, I do not want to give a god
forsaken lesson to the other party about   what in the good
name they are debating;
I have leaped as sheep to put people to bed,
thinking tires
thinking is on the road
when you learn, and I will quote George Harrison:
       *"If you don't know where you're going, any road will
take you there[1]"*

---

[1]George Harrison, Any Road, Brainwashed

and to learn who we are,
to tie our own shoes
if an oral tradition, and politics is a genetic thing,
then let me tell you this -
we are doomed.
Buying booze on a smokey street at night
there is a sonata in my head,
there is a dollar in the palm of an open handed hobo which I put there
there is a joy in the back of my head
when I will have worn his coat there are people like me
and if we lean forward on the company,
the subway restaurant is some example
on the sneeze guard you will read "do not lean on the glass"
you are heavy and so is everyone else,
could you imagine something so terrible as to
in the chimney pipes,
loose thousands of precious, earned, but forsaken work days,
a citizen with age, rests upon his cane
and the principles of such people
they did not appear so clearly to everyone.
And so I'm buying booze on a smokey street at night,
I am feeling fine
I am growing strange for I might leave soon,
my plans aren't made yet,
but Copenhagen here I come.
The beans aren't salted
my hat's been stolen, and my jacket, and I have nothing to hold
me back
my beans aren't salted,
I can now wash them down,
buying booze on a smokey street corner at night.

Do you not want her to have the love she deserves for being herself ?
And blind as you are, fighting off the suitors
and ripping the love letters, the mail they have sent
confetti thrown up in the wind,
in the discus of time passing
and being alone
missing one who would take away
gladly take away, to be the chosen bearer of confidence and care,
do you not want her to be glad?
As she receives the anticipated package
spun, the enthusiasm warms her night-like body
broken by a day to come
but for those who have been trapped by the dusk
daybreak might never arrive or be awaited in what others call a
lifetime.

Exile is thought
exile is truth
exile is knowledge
upon one's self and upon you
exile is peacefulness
and exile is a rush
as a shamble-shocked mind
rocks with the storming waves
of the wind of the weather
we go against and blow
this joint to puff about
to taste
is exile
to see further and further
with-
in upon exile
rolling hills
rising, and falling back within themselves
the earth is shaking
in exile
we meet
let our exiles combine
and share with what we have learned
and plow fields
as the hills collapse
as the hay grows
in which to lie,
to close one's eyes
or your
own
the day

which costs nothing
freedom starts with free
and living for nothing
breathing and eating
and to appreciate what
there is exile
always coming back
exile is regret
consolation
as the medicine
is the medicine
in exile
we meet,
and further down the road
before the harbour docks
there is a bench
passing by
it rains, then comes together again
lifting up their own personal exile
joining eventually, the numbers
whistling careless life
hunted down, collapsing one into the other
sharing
eventual
inevitable
exile,
exile is discovery
exile is absolute
exile is wilderness
exile is the realization of feelings
exile is coming to terms
exile is tasting every morsel

the inhaled smoke,
the exhaled breath
the cool clean air surrounding
drizzle, the sea goes on
foaming rage
appease
exile
gnaw yourself to the damned core
and take charge
of though own subject
falling in and out,
sitting on a bench
sailing the lengths of solemnity
warning under the sun
the day dreaming in reverse
of perpetual exile.

Did I dream about what you said?
I cannot recall properly
it seems
I would have to know
so much
that I've invented some
and found it out
– digging, dreaming,
roaming wild amongst the packs of orphans
enjoying such liberty
wishing for something else
being one's own family
wrestles,
have I dreamt over and over
some mumbling words I'd be quick to remember
calling for occasions to
recklessly we, our somewhere beginning
that which will always
adapt through the obvious need
to create is dangerous survival
with a blessing
they leave together to live
raising new eyes
an overflowing cup
an overwhelming toast
to all the orphans finding their own paths
with ears looking out forgetting
every sound hunting
so I can be certain
if it is, or whether it is not
that which you had said

and that I've not dreamt once more
like too often
of you

Why, my good man, you've caught me stealing!
I guess I'd better return what would have kept me warm
what would have fedd me
you've caught me begging too discretely
too shameful to ask
a hobo basking in the capacity of his own wretch
and description, and luck
I guess I'd better undo my too early feeling of victory
my drooling wide gaping mouth
white gleaming teeth to dig in
flesh of weakness, flesh of sin
where is the beginning of regret to my kind
you have caught me, dear sir
so off to the gallows.

We complete each other as you said
Allah give us our daily bread
my other half is somewhere different
and I have left you somewhere, sadly
I will join you, if we wait kindly
"nothing is ready" is the statement
I think of you both night and day
when will there be no reasons, stay
a ring on your finger, a crown
my princess I do adore
you gasp from pleasure when I go down
time of passion is but a store
I miss your eyes, I miss your person
I miss the background you give to me
yours is mine is family
draw us apart I see no reason
these sharpened pencils bear no erasers
our lives joined have seen but teasers
we complete each other, too early, too late
we can't make up no one blank slate
"nothing is ready" is the statement
time will arrange both same and different
very soon, I pray good fortune
will be together as sun to Neptune
on the horizon sets, we follow
fill in the gaps, before we're hollow

* 9 7 8 9 3 9 0 2 0 2 9 4 2 *